MEETING STANDARDS & RAISING TEST SCORES WHEN YOU DON'T HAVE MUCH TIME OR MONEY

Payne, Ruby K., & Magee, Donna S.
    Meeting Standards and Raising Test Scores When You Don't
    Have Much Time or Money. 131 pp.
    Bibliography pp. 133
    ISBN: 1-929229-17-8

1. Education   2. Reading   3. Title

RUBY K. PAYNE, PH.D.
DONNA S. MAGEE

MEETING STANDARDS & RAISING TEST SCORES WHEN YOU DON'T HAVE MUCH TIME OR MONEY

Table of Contents

Achieving Critical Mass

Issues with Current Models in Staff Development and Curriculum

1. Time frames of accountability

2. Critical mass within time frames

3. Increased amount of required knowledge for teachers

4. Accountability requirements for campus/district

to build critical mass
35–40%

To Achieve Critical Mass

1. Identify leaders (omnivores)

    a. Provide in-depth training for omnivores

    b. Enable trainees to operationalize

    c. Embed immediately into schoolwide program/calendar

2. Keep processes simple, using less time

3. Involve more people

4. Manage relationships, not people

Attitudes Towards Staff Development
(Showers & Joyce)

10%	Omnivores – like training
10%	Active receivers
70% 35% for critical mass	passive receivers – goto training only – insistence – support = be there with you
10%	reluctant receivers – just don't go to training – call in sick – leave the meeting more than not

Staff Development
Indepth vs. Accountability

expertise

1 out of 4 individuals will use
and apply the training - so be picky about
who gets to go! Get the ones who will
"operationalize" the training.

How and Who do we "operationalize" our
training to make it effective. What parts
do we select to share and implement with
the rest of the staff at a whole staff
meeting.

Identifying Belief Systems

BELIEFS AND THEIR IMPLICATIONS

Belief	Purpose of Education	Vocabulary	Method of Evaluation	Common Comments
Cognitive Processors	To teach students to think	Thinking skills, intellectual development, problem-solving	Observation of performance	"As long as they can think, it doesn't matter what we teach …"
Self-actualizers	To allow students to develop as individuals to their level of potential	Peak experience, whole child, affective, nurturance	IEP (Individualized Education Plan), holistic, developmental progression of skills	"I just want her to feel good about herself. I am not going to push her; it could harm her …"
Technologists	To have students meet set of standards and demonstrate their learning against those standards	Measurable learning, task analysis, input, output, diagnosis of systems, computers, distance learning	Pre and post tests, gain scores, growth against standardized measures	"Is he learning or not? Did he make any growth? I don't care how he feels about it …"
Academic Rationalists	To learn a discipline and be able to use that discipline	Classics; humanities; traditional curriculum; rigor; basics; scholarly, conceptual themes	Mastery of content, achievement testing, summative testing	"My job is to teach the content; his job is to learn it …"
Social Reconstruc-tionists	To nurture social conscience and look out for well-being of world now and in future	Survival, consumer education, environment, peace education	Service hours; involvement in social reconstruction activities, editorials	"What does it matter what they know if there is no longer a world to live in?"
Moral Standard Bearers	To build character and moral human beings who can participate in immoral society	Character education, moral imperatives, God and country, vouchers, charter schools, privacy	Essays, knowledge of basics and classics tested	"There is so much evil in the world. They need to learn to obey. There is no point in learning anything but the basics and the classics."
Brain-based-learning Devotees	To interact with language and environment to make meaning	Brain-based connections, making meaning, thematic curriculum, patterns	Rubrics, projects, performance assessments, identification of patterns	"If students cannot make meaning and identify patterns, why bother? Little else is remembered."
Legal Requirement	To fulfill the law	Law, truancy	Attendance	"I have to."

Adapted from the works of Eisner and Vallance, *Conflicting Conceptions of Curriculum*: McCutchan Publishing, Berkley, CA, 1974, and Mark Gerzon, *A House Divided*: Putnam Publishing Co., New York, NY, 1996.

CASE STUDY ON BELIEFS

Your leadership team is in the second year of working toward long-term improvement. One of the team's data-driven goals is to improve achievement in science. The team found that only 60% of the sixth-graders could achieve a 70% mastery level on a criterion-referenced test dealing with physical, biological, and earth sciences. In reviewing the science curriculum for grades 1 through 6, the team found that science basically consisted of whatever the teacher had time for or wanted to teach. The team has decided to have a summer project to write the science curriculum. Before this occurs, however, the team wants to have input from all staff to develop a framework of appropriate content and labs at each grade level. The fourth-grade teachers are deadlocked and cannot come to consensus.

The fourth grade has five teachers:

BETTY – is a proponent of process science. She is in her mid-40s, has been teaching for 20 years, is recently divorced, and is an anti-smoking crusader. She agrees with Pete that labs are very important but believes that his content is much too difficult for fourth-graders. Several times in meetings she and Pete have verbally "tangled." At one recent meeting Pete called Betty a "frustrated female" to which Betty retorted, "You have never successfully resolved your midlife crisis, and now you want to punish the children with useless knowledge – the only thing you can handle!" Then Betty laughed, and Pete lit a cigarette. *Self Actualized*
Academic Cog. Proc.

PETE – is in his early 50s and has been in education for 26 years. He spent some time in administration but preferred teaching, so he returned to it. His hobby is science, and he has many additional graduate hours in the subject. Pete states very strongly that the science curriculum has neglected basic concepts in chemistry, gravity, and machines (physical science), adding that those topics should be a focus in the fourth grade. Labs are very important also, he thinks, and he has written up labs that fourth-graders should do. He refers to Megan's insistence on peace education as "airhead fluff." Parents of the high-ability students speak very favorably of his teaching. *Academic/Cognitive*

JUAN – is in his early 30s, is recently married, and has been teaching seven years. He's still not sure if teaching is for him. However, his hobby is computers, and he believes that the fourth-grade curriculum should include computer-aided instruction, particularly in using some of the simulations for lab activities. (Anne, incidentally, has never touched a computer.) One of Juan's main concerns with this curriculum development is the order and sequence. At one meeting he said, "Just tell me what to do! Must we talk for hours? I want to know what Step 1 is, Step 2, etc! I'll just use my computer with whatever units you decide." Pete agrees with Juan that the lab simulations would be advantageous, specifically for some of the chemical calculations. Juan feels that, in the future curriculum, technology and science will be so integrated that students need to learn them together now. *Tech*

MEGAN – is recently out of college, is in her early 20s, and has been teaching for two years. She feels very deeply that peace education (anti-nuclear) should be a part of the science curriculum and has spent considerable time lobbying for this unit. She admits that science "is not my thing" and feels that social issues related to science are more important. As she says, "What good is science if you don't understand how it affects people and the way they live?" Megan believes curriculum should be both relevant and fun: "After all, my parents (a doctor and a lawyer) spent 16 hours a day working. Life should be fun!" *Social Rec.* *Self Act.*

ANNE – is in her early 40s, has two young children, 8 and 10, and has been teaching for 15 years. It's her strong belief that the science curriculum should include what is appropriate for the child. After looking at Pete's sample labs, she commented privately to Juan, "I don't understand them. How could the children? If that's what they decide on, I don't know how I would ever do them!" Anne would like to see units on plants and animals because students become attached to them in a positive way. As Anne said in the meeting, "I just want the kids to feel good about science." Anne has missed two after-school meetings – once for an orthodontist appointment and once for a piano recital, both of which involved her children. Anne also told the principal that she's embarrassed by Pete and Betty's name-calling, saying, "I just don't think people should talk to each other that way." She's reluctant to go to any more meetings. *Moral St.* *Self Act.*

QUESTIONS:

1. What are the prevalent belief systems and who represents them? – *Give up the "love units"* *① Identify the standards. ② Revisit operational norms.*

2. What compromises might the fourth-grade teachers make to arrive at a curriculum which they all could teach?

3. What can you as a leadership team do to meet these two objectives?

   a. Arrive at a set of curriculum topics that would be taught at that grade level.

   b. Assist the team in working together.

Glickman's Grid

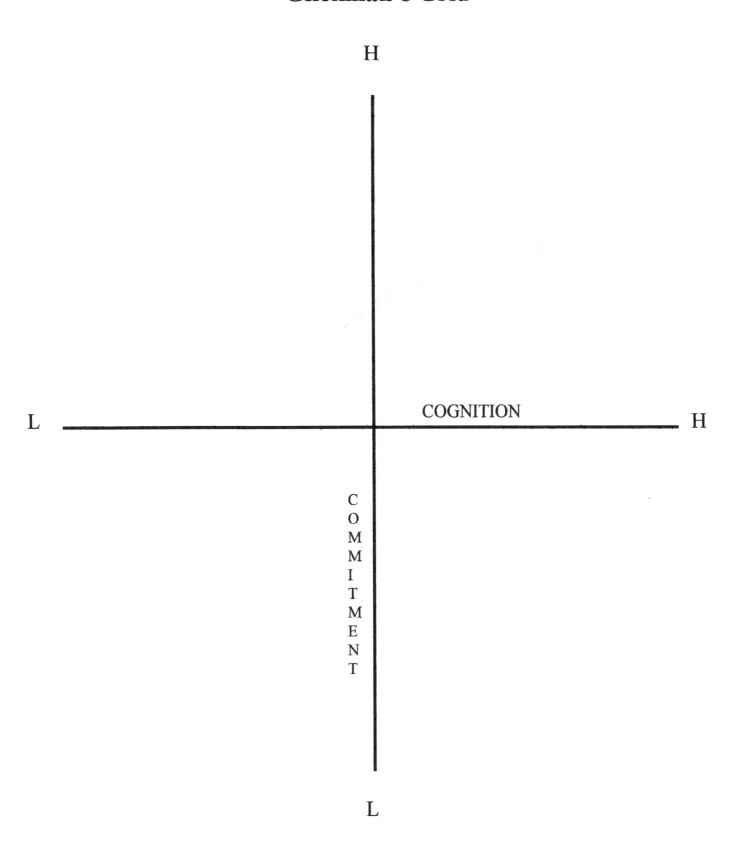

Characteristics of Age

(Adapted from Judy-Arin Krupp)

Age	Characteristics	Strategy/Best Role
18-29		
28-32		
30's		
38-42		
40's		
50 and up		

IMPLEMENTING THE FIVE PROCESSES

Process 1: Identifying Students by Quartile

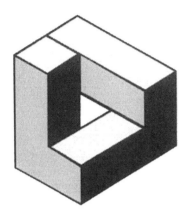

Simple exercise to:
1. Predict assessment rating
2. Address equity issues – note subgroups not served
3. Identify specific students to target
4. Enable timely intervention

Quartile	Native American	Hispanic	African American	Asian	Caucasian	Low Socio-Economic Status	LEP*	Disabled
75-100%								
50-74%								
25-49%								
0-24%								

*(limited English proficiency)

Tracking student progress by quartile helps measure student growth and determine the amount of progress that is probable in a given year. It helps us determine how many students, and specifically which students, we need to move.

Prediction guide: To achieve 80% passing on state assessment, 80% of students must score above 50% on normed reference test.

GRADE LEVEL: CIRCLE ONE: READING   MATH

TEST BAND	African American	Hispanic	Caucasian	Low Socio-Economic Status	Limited English Proficiency	Disabled
75-100%	**In this block write the name of any African American student who had a score of 75 % or higher**	**Any Hispanic student who had a score of 75% or higher**				
50-74%	**Write the name of any African American student who had a score of 50-74%**					
25-49%	**Write the name of any African American student who had a score of 25-49%**					
0-24%						
Students who were exempt						

Adapt this chart to the subgroups present in your school.

Steps to grid students by quartile:

Whether your state uses a norm-referenced or criterion-referenced test does not matter.

Step 1: Put the names of students in each box based on ethnicity and percentile scores. Students of low socio-economic status should be counted in both ethnic group and low socio-economic status. Each teacher does this for the students he/she teaches; at the elementary level, one grid is completed for reading and one for math, if both subject areas are tested. At the secondary level, teachers complete it for the subject area, math or English, that they teach.

Step 2: Identify the school patterns by gathering numbers from each teacher's grid and then make predictions based on number of students in each quartile.

Step 3: Analyze individual students in each quartile and decide which students can be moved to the next higher quartile in one year based upon specific interventions. It is important that no student stay in the same quartile more than two years; the student will simply not make necessary growth if he/she remains in the same quartile more than two years.

     Meeting Standards & Raising Test Scores • **aha!** Process, Inc. • www.ahaprocess.com

GRADE LEVEL: CIRCLE ONE: READING   MATH

TEST BAND	African American	Hispanic	Caucasian	Low Socio-Economic Status	Limited English Proficiency	Disabled
75-100%						
50-74%						
25-49%						
0-24%						
Students who are exempt						

Adapt this chart to the subgroups present in your school.

GRADE LEVEL: CIRCLE ONE: READING   MATH

TEST BAND	African American	Hispanic	Caucasian	Low Socio-Economic Status	Limited English Proficiency	Disabled
75-100%						
50-74%						
25-49%						
0-24%						
Students who are exempt						

Adapt this chart to the subgroups present in your school

Meeting Standards & Raising Test Scores • **aha!** Process, Inc. • www.ahaprocess.com

GRADE LEVEL: CIRCLE ONE: READING   MATH

TEST BAND	African American	Hispanic	Caucasian	Low Socio-Economic Status	Limited English Proficiency	Disabled
75-100%						
50-74%						
25-49%						
0-24%						
Students who are exempt						

Adapt this chart to the subgroups present in your school

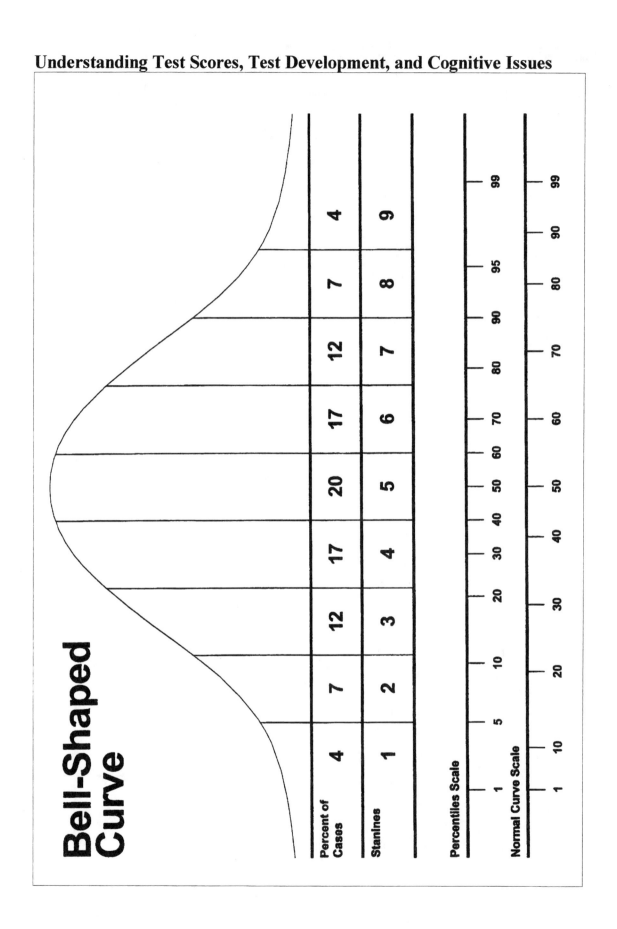

Bell-Shaped Curve

Percent of Cases	4	7	12	17	20	17	12	7	4
Stanines	1	2	3	4	5	6	7	8	9
Percentiles Scale	1	5	10	20	30	40	50	60	70	80	90	95	99
Normal Curve Scale	1	10	20	30	40	50	60	70	80	90	99

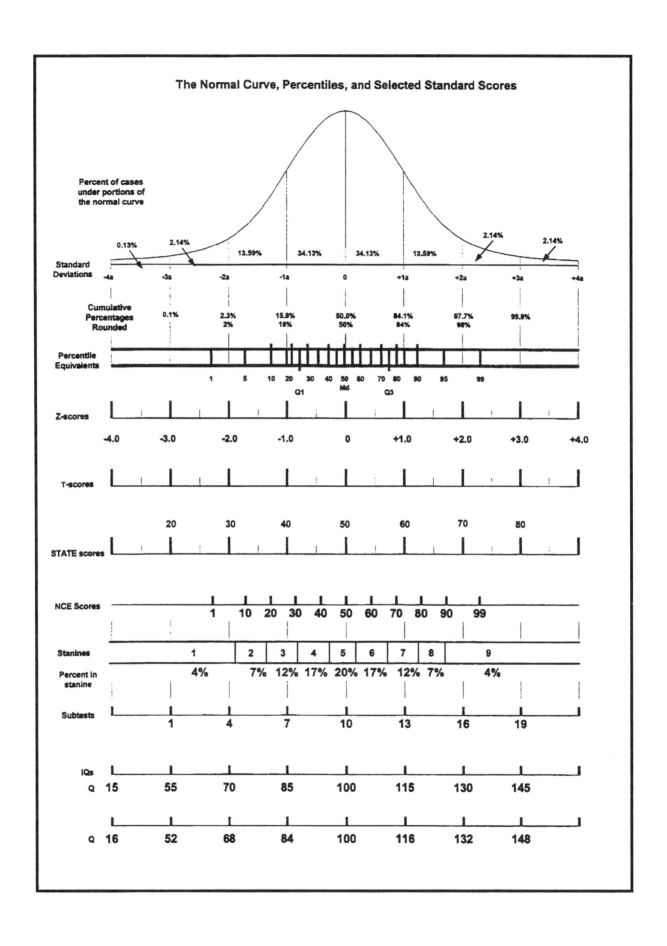

The Normal Curve, Percentiles, and Selected Standard Scores

EFFECTIVE SCHOOL

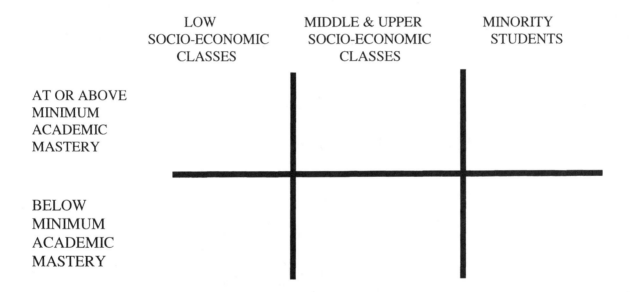

	LOW SOCIO-ECONOMIC CLASSES	MIDDLE & UPPER SOCIO-ECONOMIC CLASSES	MINORITY STUDENTS
AT OR ABOVE MINIMUM ACADEMIC MASTERY			
BELOW MINIMUM ACADEMIC MASTERY			

Process 2: Assigning Time and Aligning Instruction

We must know what we are teaching.

How much time equals what payoff?

We must know what we will teach and why.

Improving Test Scores and Student Achievement

Four factors that make a difference in learning and student achievement:

1. Amount of time spent.

2. Clarity of focus of instruction.

3. What the student came in knowing.

4. Intervention of teacher.

–Benjamin Bloom

What is being taught?

First Nine Weeks	Second Nine Weeks

Third Nine Weeks	Fourth Nine Weeks

Meeting Standards & Raising Test Scores • **aha!** Process, Inc. • www.ahaprocess.com

First Six Weeks	Second Six Weeks	Third Six Weeks

Fourth Six Weeks	Fifth Six Weeks	Sixth Six Weeks

Steps in the Process of Identifying 'the What'

1. **Write current curriculum.** Each teacher writes down on <u>one page per subject</u> what he/she is currently teaching and for how long. Either of the examples listed previously may be used, or design your own.

2. **Teachers meet by grade level or department.** All teachers at each grade level/department get together and identify, on one page per subject, what SHOULD happen. Teachers bring their own papers from Step 1, their test data, and state standards, and then come to a consensus. (Use roving substitute teacher to enable meetings.)

3. **Hold building-level faculty meeting.** Everyone in the building gets together, and each teacher has a copy of all the grade levels by subject. Discussion focuses on the opportunities of the student to learn. Where are the gaps and holes? Align curriculum vertically throughout the grades. This enables teachers to determine the primary focus of what will be taught.

4. **A subcommittee revises the documents.** Based on the discussion, a subcommittee revises the documents in preparation for implementation.

5. **The instructional units are keyed to the standards.**

   Do this at the beginning of each year – everyone knows what to teach, and it really helps new teachers.

Examples of work done by a school(s) to complete this "aligning time and aligning instruction" process follow in the manual.

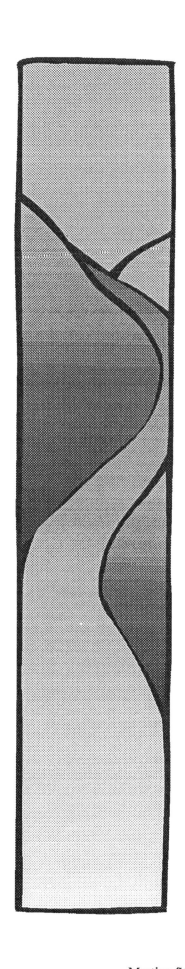

Reasonable Expectations

**Developed by the Faculty of
Runyan Elementary, Grades 1-4
Conroe, Texas**

Principal: Nancy Harris

**(Using Aligning Time and
Aligning Instruction Exercise)**

FIRST-GRADE MATH CURRICULUM

FIRST SIX WEEKS

Patterning

Attributes

Conserve numbers to 3

1-to-1 correspondence

Odd/even

SECOND SIX WEEKS

Graphing (all)

More/less

Measurements

Ordinals

Compare objects

THIRD SIX WEEKS

Part to whole (½)

Number sense

Addition (1 digit)

Story problems (direct-teach)

Place value (10's and 1's)

FOURTH SIX WEEKS

Skip counting (2, 5, 10)

Money (1 cent & 5 cents)

Shapes (circle, square, triangle, cube, cone, pyramid)

FIFTH SIX WEEKS

Addition (2 digits)

Subtraction (1 digit)

SIXTH SIX WEEKS

Number words to 20

Greatest to least/least to greatest

Place value

SECOND-GRADE MATH CURRICULUM
60 MINUTES DAILY

FIRST SIX WEEKS

Number line – 2 weeks
    Least to greatest/greatest to least
    Odd & even
    Skip counting by 10, 4, 2
    Before, after, between
    Ordinal numbers – 1st through 20th

Problem solving – 1 week
    (continued throughout year)

Addition & subtraction – 1½ weeks
    Fact families
    Word problems

SECOND SIX WEEKS

Place value – 2 weeks
    1, 10, 100
    Expanded notation
    Counting & writing to 100

Addition without regrouping – 2½ weeks
    2 & 3 digits
    Word problems

Estimation & rounding – 1½ weeks
    (continued throughout year)
    Word problems

THIRD SIX WEEKS

Addition
    With regrouping – 2 & 3 digits –
        2½ weeks
    Word problems

Measurement – 1 week
    Length
    Capacity
    Weight
    Standard vs. non-standard units
    Word problems

FOURTH SIX WEEKS

Subtraction
    Without regrouping – 2 & 3 digits –
        1 week
    With regrouping – 2 & 3 digits –
        2½ weeks
    Word problems

FIFTH SIX WEEKS

Time – 2 weeks
    1 hour, ½ hour, ¼ hour with word problems

Money – 2½ weeks
    Value of coins: 1, 5, 10, 25 cents & $1
    Adding coins
    Subtracting coins
    Word problems

Introduce probability & statistics – 1½ weeks

SIXTH SIX WEEKS

Fractions – 1 week
    Name & identify fractional parts
    Compare

Geometry – 1 week
    Solids
    Congruent
    Symmetry

Probability & statistics – 1 week

Introduce multiplication – 1½ weeks

THIRD-GRADE MATH CURRICULUM
60 MINUTES DAILY

FIRST SIX WEEKS

Problem-solving process

Math journals

Place value to 4 digits (thousandths introduced)

Reading/writing 4-digit numbers

Compare & order numbers

Multiplication & subtraction with trades,
    including 3 digits

SECOND SIX WEEKS

Multiplication facts

Add/subtract 4 digits with trades, including 0's

Customary measurements

Column addition – 2 & 3 digits

Rounding/estimation

Ongoing
    Math journals
    Graphing
    Problem-solving
    Estimation

THIRD SIX WEEKS

Multiplication extended – 2 digits x 1 digit

Fractions

Metric measurement

Calculators

FOURTH SIX WEEKS

Time elapsed – a.m./p.m.

Money

Multiplication (continued)

Decimals

FIFTH SIX WEEKS

Geometry

Probability & statistics

Gridding

SIXTH SIX WEEKS

Division

Gridding (continued)

Probability & statistics

FOURTH-GRADE MATH CURRICULUM
60 MINUTES DAILY

FIRST SIX WEEKS

Place value to million

Reading/writing 6-digit numbers

Compare & order numbers 1 to 6 digits

Rounding 10, 100, 1,000

Whole numbers & money

Adding & subtracting up to 4 digits with trades

Problem-solving steps

Ongoing
    Math journals
    Graphing
    Problem-solving
    Estimation with 6-weeks concepts

SECOND SIX WEEKS

Adding & subtracting 6 digits with trades,
    including 0's

Column addition

Metric measurement
    Volume
    Mass
    Linear

Calculators

Multiplication (all 6 weeks) facts, 0-9

THIRD SIX WEEKS

Fractions

Customary measurement
    Volume
    Mass
    Linear

Multiplication: 2 places x 2 places

FOURTH SIX WEEKS

Division
    Facts & single-digit divisor & remainders

Time elapsed

Money

FIFTH SIX WEEKS

Geometry

Probability & statistics

SIXTH SIX WEEKS

Fractions
    Common denominator
    Division & subtraction
    Greater, less, equal

2-digit divisors

Long division

FIFTH-GRADE MATH CURRICULUM
60 MINUTES DAILY

FIRST SIX WEEKS

Number concepts – whole number and decimals
    Compare and order
        Whole numbers – ones to billions
        Decimals – tenth, hundredths and thousandths
    Place value 1 to 12 digits
    Rounding
    Number lines
Estimation/solution sentences/reasonableness
    Estimation: whole numbers and money
Problem solving using addition, subtraction, division
        and multiplication (and estimation of these)
Mathematical relation and representation
    Inverse operations/fact families
    Formulate solution sentences
    Algebraic thinking
Mastery of all basic facts
Problem solving
Problem of the day
Reasonableness and Estimation

SECOND SIX WEEKS

Problem Solving Operations: addition, subtraction
    multiplication and division using whole numbers
    and decimals
Estimation, mathematical relations/reasonableness
    Formulate solution sentences

Number Concepts
    Prime and composite numbers
    Factoring whole numbers
    Greatest common factor and least common multiple
    Divisibility rates
Fractions
    Equivalent fractions
    Compare and order fractions
    Number lines with fractions
Mastery of all basic facts
Problem solving strategies
Problem of the day
Reasonableness and Estimation

THIRD SIX WEEKS

Geometry
    Lines, Points Angles,
    2-and 3-dimensional figures
    Congruent figures, lines of symmetry
    Parts of a circle
    Transformations
    Coordinate planes

Solution strategies

Geometry measurement
    Perimeter, area, circumference, volume

Problem of the day continued
Review problem-solving strategies

FOURTH SIX WEEKS

Measurement
    Metric and customary conversions with
        problem solving
    Weight/mass, capacity
    Time
    Length, perimeter
Probability/statistics with solution strategies
    Ratio, mean, median, range
    Possible outcomes
    Fractions to describe events
    Fractional probability / problem solving
    Probability using situations / problem solving
Review problem-solving strategies
Problem of the day
Reasonableness and estimation

FIFTH SIX WEEKS

Counting arrangements
Combinations
Graphs, charts, tables
Estimation
Whole numbers money using addition, subtraction
    multiplication, division

SIXTH SIX WEEKS

Review and reteach objectives where needed

Give practice tests
Review problems solving strategies
Expose students to new items they may encounter
    on tests

Adapted from Goose Creek Consolidated Independent School District, Mathematics Scope & Sequence, Grade 5

FIRST-GRADE WRITING AND SPELLING CURRICULUM

FIRST SIX WEEKS

Concepts of writing
    Top to bottom
    Left to right
    Beginning sound of words
    Relate orally an original illustration
    Vocabulary

SECOND SIX WEEKS

Invented spelling, using initial and final
    sound

Identify beginnings of sentences

Show evidence of use of new vocabulary in
    writing

Appropriate use of lower-case letters; does
    not use all caps

Use appropriate spacing between words

THIRD SIX WEEKS

Show evidence of use of vowels in writing

Show evidence of use of punctuation

Begin using words that show action

Show evidence of invented spelling in
    writing, using correct beginning-,
    ending-, and middle-sound family
    words

FOURTH SIX WEEKS

Write 1 simple-sentence story, using
    appropriate-conventions subject,
    adverb, adjective

Concepts of narrative

Use new vocabulary in daily writing

Special C-V-C 60 words
    (continued through year; same number of
    words, but pattern changes)

FIFTH SIX WEEKS

Write 1- or 2-sentence story, using appropriate
    conventions

Concepts of telling sentence (.)

Concepts of how-to

Continue concepts of narrative

Use new vocabulary in daily writing

SIXTH SIX WEEKS

Write 2- or 3- sentence story, using appropriate
    conventions

Concepts of asking sentence (?)

Concepts of descriptive

Continue concepts of narrative and how-to

Use new vocabulary in daily writing

SECOND-GRADE LANGUAGE ARTS CURRICULUM
70% FICTION, 30% NON-FICTION

FIRST SIX WEEKS

READING – 60 minutes
DEAR (Drop Everything and
   Read) – 10 minutes
Teacher reading to students
Reading workshop – 50 minutes

SPELLING – 15 minutes
   60 words
10 words per week

WRITING – 45 minutes
Personal narrative: 2-3
   sentences on same subject
DOL (Daily Oral Language) –
   15 minutes
Writing workshop – 30
   minutes

VOCABULARY – integrated
5 words per week

SKILLS – 20 minutes
Choosing just right books
Characters
Predicting
Distinguishing between fiction
   and non-fiction

SECOND SIX WEEKS

READING – 60 minutes
DEAR – 10 minutes
Teacher reading to students
Reading workshop – 50 minutes

SPELLING – 15 minutes
   60 words
10 words per week

WRITING – 45 minutes
6-7 lines on same subject for
   how-to
DOL – 15 minutes
Writing workshop – 30
   minutes

VOCABULARY – integrated
5 words per week

SKILLS – 20 minutes
Setting
Beginning, middle, end of story
Parts of speech: noun, verb
Sequential order
Comprehension
Compound words
Contractions

THIRD SIX WEEKS

Reading – 60 minutes
DEAR – 10 minutes
Teacher reading to students
Reading workshop – 50 minutes

SPELLING – 15 minutes
   60 words
10 words per week

WRITING – 45 minutes
5-7 steps in paragraph,
   sequential for how-to
DOL – 15 minutes
Writing workshop – 30
   minutes

VOCABULARY – integrated
5 words per week

SKILLS – 20 minutes
Main idea
Prefixes, suffixes
Context clues
Synonyms, antonyms,
   homophones, homonyms
Comprehension
Compound words
Contractions

SECOND-GRADE LANGUAGE ARTS CURRICULUM (continued)
70% FICTION, 30% NON-FICTION

FOURTH SIX WEEKS

READING – 60 minutes
DEAR – 15 minutes
Teacher reading to students
Reading workshop – 45 minutes

SPELLING – 15 minutes
    60 words
10 words per week
ABC order to second letter

WRITING – 45 minutes
How-to: 5-7 steps in paragraph
    form
DOL – 15 minutes, TAAS (Texas
    Assessment of Academic
    Skills) form
Writing workshop – 30 minutes

VOCABULARY – integrated
5 words per week

SKILLS – 20 minutes
Uses quotes
Draws conclusions
Makes inferences
Adjectives, adverbs
Comprehension
Possessives
Compound words
Contractions

FIFTH SIX WEEKS

READING – 60 minutes
DEAR – 15 minutes
Teacher reading to students
Reading workshop – 45 minutes

SPELLING – 15 minutes
    60 words
10 words per week
ABC order to third letter

WRITING – 45 minutes
Descriptive writing – 7 sentences
Compare/contrast
DOL – 15 minutes, TAAS form
Writing workshop – 30 minutes

VOCABULARY – integrated
5 words per week

SKILLS – 20 minutes
Main idea distinguished from details
Fact/opinion
Cause/effect
Comprehension
Possessives
Compound words
Contractions

SIXTH SIX WEEKS

Reading – 60 minutes
DEAR – 15 minutcs
Teacher reading to students
Reading workshop – 45 minutes

SPELLING – 15 minutes
    60 words
10 words per week
ABC order to third letter

WRITING – 45 minutes
Summary
Compare/contrast
DOL – 15 minutes, TAAS form
Writing workshop – 30 minutes

VOCABULARY – integrated
5 words per week

SKILLS – 20 minutes
Recognizes propaganda and point
    of view
Comprehension
Possessives
Compound words
Contractions

THIRD-GRADE LANGUAGE ARTS CURRICULUM
50% FICTION, 50% NON-FICTION

FIRST SIX WEEKS

READING – 30 minutes SSR
   (Sustained Silent Reading)
Journals and reading response
   logs – 30 minutes
Skills
   Using context skills
   Mapping and webbing
   Building vocabulary
      (word meaning)

SPELLING – 10-15 minutes
10 words per week – high frequency
   words

WRITING – 45 minutes
15-minute mini-lesson
Writer's notebook
Descriptive writing
Sentences – developing fluency

VOCABULARY –
   integrated
5 words per week

SECOND SIX WEEKS

READING – 30 minutes SSR
Journals and reading-response
   logs – 30 minutes
Skills
   Summarizing
   Context clues
   Drawing conclusions
   Predicting

SPELLING – 10-15 minutes
10 words per week – high-frequency
   words

WRITING – 45 minutes
15-minute mini-lesson
Personal and expressive narrative
Language awareness
Reasons for writing
Developing frequency

VOCABULARY –
   integrated
5 words per week

THIRD SIX WEEKS

Reading – 30 minutes SSR
Journals and reading-response
   logs – 30 minutes
Tall tales (reading/writing)
Comprehension skills
Relationships and outcomes
Inferences and generalizations
Compound words

SPELLING – 10- 15 minutes
10 words per week – high-frequency
   words

WRITING – 45 minutes
15-minute mini-lesson
How-to
Editing skills introduced

VOCABULARY –
   integrated
5 words per week

FOURTH SIX WEEKS

READING – 45 minutes SSR
15 minutes – other
Cause/effect
Compare and contrast
Fact and non-fact (opinion)
Recalling facts and details
Supporting ideas

SPELLING – 10-15 minutes
10 words per week – high-
   frequency words

WRITING – 45 minutes
15-minute mini-lesson
Classificatory
Verbs

VOCABULARY – integrated
5 words per week

FIFTH SIX WEEKS

READING – 60 minutes SSR
Point of view and propaganda
Main idea
Drawing conclusions
Finding and highlighting

SPELLING – 10-15 minutes
10 words per week – high-
   frequency words

WRITING – 45 minutes
15-minute mini-lesson
Persuasive
Share writing in variety of formats

VOCABULARY – integrated
5 words per week

SIXTH SIX WEEKS

READING – 60 minutes SSR

SPELLING – 10-15 minutes
10 words per week – high-
   frequency words

WRITING – 45 minutes
15-minute mini-lesson
Biographies
Use CD-ROM, computer catalog
Reference material
Note taking

VOCABULARY – integrated
5 words per week

FOURTH-GRADE LANGUAGE ARTS CURRICULUM
50% FICTION, 50% NON-FICTION

FIRST SIX WEEKS

READING – 20-minute mini-lesson; 60-minute SSR
Prefixes and suffixes
Antonyms and synonyms
Figurative and literal

SPELLING – 15 minutes
10 words per week – high-frequency words

WRITING – 15-minute mini-lesson; 30-minute process writing
Descriptive writing, poetry
Complete sentences
Fragments and run-ons
Capitalization and punctuation

VOCABULARY – introduce 10, responsible for 5

SKILLS – 15- TO 20-minute DOL (Daily Oral Language)

SECOND SIX WEEKS

READING – 20-minute mini-lesson; 60-minute SSR
Story structure
 Setting
 Characterization
 Point of view
 Feelings and emotions of
  characters

SPELLING – 15 minutes
10 words per week – high-frequency words

WRITING – 15-minutes mini-lesson; 30 minute process writing
Narrative and keyboarding
Subjects, objects, and
 possessive forms of pronouns
Subject/verb agreement with
 personal pronouns and
 compound subjects with
 expressed and unexpressed
 subjects

VOCABULARY – introduce 10, responsible for 5
SKILLS – 15- to 20-minute DOL

THIRD SIX WEEKS

READING – 20-minute mini-lesson; 60-minute SSR
Context clues
Fact and detail
Sequencing

SPELLING – 15 minutes
10 words per week – high-frequency words

WRITING – 15-minute mini-lesson; 30-minute process writing
How-to
Verb tenses
Irregular verbs

VOCABULARY – introduce 10, responsible for 5

SKILLS – 15- to 20-minute DOL

FOURTH SIX WEEKS

READING – 20-minute mini-lesson; 60-minute SSR
Main idea
Summarizing
Paraphrasing

SPELLING – 15 minutes
10 words per week – high-frequency words

WRITING – 15-minute mini-lesson; 30-minute process writing
Classificatory
Adjectives, adverbs
Combine sentence parts
 (Objective 5)

VOCABULARY – introduce 10, responsible for 5

SKILLS – 15- to 20-minute DOL

FIFTH SIX WEEKS

READING – 20-minute mini-lesson; 60-minute SSR
Cause/effect
Draw conclusions
Predict outcomes
Use graphic sources
Fact and non-fact, opinion

SPELLING – 15 minutes
10 words per week – high-frequency words

WRITING – 15-minute mini-lesson; 30-minute process writing
Persuasive

VOCABULARY – introduce 10, responsible for 5

SKILLS – 15- to 20-minute DOL

SIXTH SIX WEEKS

READING – 20-minute mini-lesson; 60-minute SSR
Novel study
Literature groups

SPELLING – 15 minutes
10 words per week – high-frequency words

WRITING – 15-minute mini-lesson; 30-minute process writing
Putting together showcase
 portfolios

VOCABULARY – introduce 10, responsible for 5

Reasonable Expectations

Language Arts Curriculum
Grade 5

Goose Creek Consolidated Independent School District
Baytown, Texas

Language Arts Scope and Sequence
Grade 5 – First Six Weeks

Reading	Grammar	Writing	Spelling	Vocabulary	Handwriting	Project Read	Listening/ Speaking
Cover each TAAS objective according to campus calendar. Assessments will be given based on calendar as well. Please Note: Teachers will listen to each student read orally 1-2 times weekly. This should be done as part of regular reading and classroom instruction. See attached chart for correlating TAAS targets and reading instruction.	**Parts of Speech** Nouns Verbs **Usage** Agreement Verb Tense **Sentence Construction** Identify: - Complete sentences - Run-on sentences - Sentence fragments **Capitalization** First word in a sentence The pronoun "I" Proper nouns **Punctuation** All end punctuation Commas - Between words in a series - Between day and year in date - Between city and state **Written Expression** Subject Predicate Linking and helping verbs	**Daily Writing** - journals - story summaries - article reviews - etc. **TAAS Focus** Persuasive **Research** Weekly class discussion on current events, film reviews, campus happenings, etc. Research must be done during the year. You may choose which six-week period in which to complete task. Use GCCISD rubrics and organizers for scoring and planning writing. See GCCISD Research Guide for activities.	**Week 1 Skills** Doubling when adding vowel suffixes that end with one vowel and consonant **Week 2 Skills** Adding suffixes to words ending in silent e **Week 3 Skills** Adding suffixes to words ending in y **Week 4 Skills** Short-vowel sounds Consonant blends and clusters **Week 5 Skills** -ck, -tch, -dge, -ss, -ll, -ff, -zz **Week 6 Skills** Closed syllable v c / c v See GCCISD Spelling Guide for words and activities.	Unit 1 abbreviate abstract articulate chalice congregate debutante elation filibuster indifferent integrity meddle paralegal posterior preclude prolific See GCCISD Vocabulary Guide for activities and assessments.	Teach all basic strokes and cursive. Review Formal heading. Please Note: 80% of all written student work should be done in cursive. See GCCISD Handwriting Guide for activities.	Emphasize Report Form completing at least one lesson a week. See Report Form Guide for activities and passages.	Weekly listening and speaking activities may include: - Teacher-selected materials - Journal responses - Current events - Oral presentations - Listening activity tapes (Learn to Listen)
Objective Assessments based on calendar	Objective Assessments based on calendar		Weekly Tests	Unit 1 Assessment			

Language Arts Scope and Sequence
Grade 5 – Second Six Weeks

Reading	Grammar	Writing	Spelling	Vocabulary	Handwriting	Project Read	Listening/Speaking
Cover each TAAS objective according to campus calendar. Assessments will be given based on calendar as well. Please Note: Teachers will listen to each student read orally 1-2 times weekly. This should be done as part of regular reading and classroom instruction. See attached chart for correlating TAAS targets and reading instruction.	**Parts of Speech** Pronouns **Usage** Pronouns Verb Tense **Sentence Construction** Identify: - Complete sentences - Run-on sentences - Sentence fragments **Capitalization** Letter opening First word in letter closing **Punctuation** Commas: - After friendly letter opening - After letter closing Apostrophes in contractions **Written Expression** Subject describers Predicate Expanders Substitute namers Prepositions Connectors Direct Objects	**Daily Writing** - journals - story summaries - article reviews - etc. **TAAS Focus** Classificatory **Research** Weekly class discussion on current events, film reviews, campus happenings, etc. Research must be done during the year. You may choose which six-week period in which to complete task. Use GCCISD rubrics and organizers for scoring and planning writing. See GCCISD Research guide for activities.	**Week 7 Skills** th, wh, ch, -tch, sh **Week 8 Skills** Open-syllable v **Week 9 Skills** v	c	v **Week 10 Skills** schwa ∂/u/ **Week 11 Skills** v c / c c v v c / c c c v **Week 12 Skills** Final-consonant le Syllable -cle See GCCISD Spelling Guide for words and activities.	Unit 1 abduct abundant belated commute concede defer exasperate fraud indivisible irreverent melody parasite postscript preclude prominent See GCCISD Vocabulary Guide for activities and assessments.	Review cursive writing through daily writing instruction Directly teach strokes, letter formation, and heading as needed. Please Note: 80% of all written student work should be done in cursive. See GCCISD Handwriting Guide for activities.	Emphasize Story Form completing at least one lesson a week. See Story Form Guide for activities and passages.	Weekly listening and speaking activities may include: - Teacher-selected materials - Journal responses - Current Events - Oral presentations - Listening activity tapes (Learn to Listen)
Fall Assessment Objective Assessments based on calendar year	Fall Assessment Objective Assessments based on calendar	Fall Assessment	Weekly Tests	Unit 2 Assessment			

Language Arts Scope and Sequence
Grade 5 – Third Six Weeks

Reading	Grammar	Writing	Spelling	Vocabulary	Handwriting	Project Read	Listening/ Speaking
Cover each TAAS objective according to campus calendar. Assessments will be given based on calendar as well.	**Parts of speech** Adverbs Conjunctions **Usage** Adjectives Verb Tense Review **Sentence Construction** Identify: - Combine sentence parts and sentences to produce a variety of structures - Construct sentences (simple, compound, complex) **Capitalization** Title used with last name Title of written work Seasons Cardinal directions **Punctuation** Commas: - Before conjunction in compound sentence Apostrophes in possessives	**Daily Writing** - journals - story summaries - article reviews - etc. **TAAS Focus** Classificatory **Research** Weekly class discussion on current events, film reviews, campus happenings, etc. Research must be done during the year. You may choose which six-week period in which to complete task. Use GCCISD rubrics and organizers for scoring and planning writing.	**Week 13 Skills** ar̆ **Week 14 Skills** er̆, ĭr, ŭr **Week 15 Skills** or̆ **Week 16 Skills** Final vowel Consonant c̲ Syllable (-vce) **Week 17 Skills** o̲i̲ and o̲y̲ **Week 18 Skills** e̲e̲ and e̲a̲ = /e/	**Unit 1** abhor acne belligerent complacent concoct defiant excruciating frond infallible keen mishap peripheral posttest prescribe promotion	Review cursive writing through daily writing instruction Directly teach strokes, letter formation, and heading as needed. Please Note: 80% of all written student work should be done in cursive.	Emphasize Story Form completing at least one lesson a week.	Weekly listening and speaking activities may include: - Teacher-selected materials - Journal responses - Current events - Oral presentations - Listening activity tapes (Learn to Listen)
Please Note: Teachers will listen to each student read orally 1-2 times weekly. This should be done as part of regular reading and classroom instruction. See attached chart for correlating TAAS targets and reading instruction.	**Written Expression** Review Written Expression through composition writing	See GCCISD Research Guide for activities.	See GCCISD Spelling Guide for words and activities.	See GCCISD Vocabulary Guide for activities and assessments.	See GCCISD Handwriting Guide for activities.	See Story Form Guide for activities and passages.	
Objective Assessments based on calendar year	Objective Assessments based on calendar year		Weekly Tests	Unit 3 Assessment			

Language Arts Scope and Sequence
Grade 5 – Fourth Six Weeks

Reading	Grammar	Writing	Spelling	Vocabulary	Handwriting	Project Read	Listening/ Speaking
Cover each TAAS objective according to campus calendar. Assessments will be given based on calendar as well. Please Note: Teachers will listen to each student read orally 1-2 times weekly. This should be done as part of regular reading and classroom instruction. See attached chart for correlating TAAS targets and reading instruction.	**Parts of Speech** Adverbs Interjections **Usage** Adverbs Pronoun Review **Sentence Construction** Identify: - Combine sentence parts and sentences to produce a variety of structures - Construct sentences (simple, compound, complex) **Capitalization** First word in quotation Family members School subjects **Punctuation** Commas: - Before direct quotation Quotation marks in quotes **Written Expression** Review Written Expression through composition writing	**Daily Writing** - journals - story summaries - article reviews - etc. **TAAS Focus** Review all modes. **Research** Weekly class discussion on current events, film reviews, campus happenings, etc. Research must be done during the year. You may choose which six-week period in which to complete task. Use GCCISD rubrics and organizers for scoring and planning writing. See GCCISD Research Guide for activities.	**Week 19 Skills** ie̱ = /a̱/ e̱y = /e/ **Week 20 Skills** e̱a = /a̱/ e̱i = /a̱/ **Week 21 Skills** o̱a = /fl/ **Week 22 Skills** o̱w = /ŏ/ o̱e = /fl/ **Week 23 Skills** Condition for y̱ as a vowel **Week 24 Skills** Soft sound of c̱ and g See GCCISD Spelling Guide for words and activities.	Unit 1 abridge adage bellow comprehend condolence delight exploit imperative infamous labyrinth mollusk permission precarious presume propeller See GCCISD Vocabulary Guide for activities and assessments.	Review cursive writing through daily writing instruction Directly teach letter strokes, letter formation, and heading as needed. Please Note: 80% of all written student work should be done in cursive. See GCCISD Handwriting Guide for activities.	Review Report Form and Story Form. See Story Form and Report Form Guide for activities and passages.	Weekly listening and speaking activities may include: - Teacher-selected materials - Journal responses - Current events - Oral presentations - Listening activity tapes (Learn to Listen)
Objective Assessments based on calendar year	Objective Assessments based on calendar year		Weekly Tests	Unit 4 Assessment			

Language Arts Scope and Sequence
Grade 5 – Fifth Six Weeks

Reading	Grammar	Writing	Spelling	Vocabulary	Handwriting	Project Read	Listening/ Speaking
Cover each TAAS objective according to campus calendar. Assessments will be given based on calendar as well.

Please Note:

Teachers will listen to each student read orally 1-2 times weekly. This should be done as part of regular reading and classroom instruction.

See attached chart for correlating TAAS targets and reading instruction. | **Parts of Speech**

Prepositions

Usage
Review and practice Usage rules using TAAS formatted pages and through composition writing.

Sentence Construction
Review and practice Sentence Construction using TAAS formatted pages and through composition writing.

Capitalization
Review and practice Capitalization rules using TAAS formatted pages and through composition writing.

Punctuation
Review and practice Punctuation rules using TAAS formatted pages and through composition writing.

Written Expression
Review Written Expression through composition writing. | **Daily Writing**
- journals
- story summaries
- article reviews
- etc.

TAAS Focus
Review all modes.

Research
Weekly class discussion on current events, film reviews, campus happenings, etc.

Research must be done during the year. You may choose which six-week period in which to complete task.

Use GCCISD rubrics and organizers for scoring and planning writing.

See GCCISD Research guide for activities. | **Week 25 Skills**

oi and oy

Week 26 Skills

ou, -ow

Week 27 Skills

oo

Week 28 Skills

-ew, -ue, -ui

Week 29 Skills

ou, -ow, ough

Week 30 Skills

oo as in look

See GCCISD Spelling Guide for words and activities. | Unit 1

abscess

adopt

cadence

comprehension

conduct

demote

extraneous

inaugurate

insipid

lavish

paradigm

persistent

precede

prodigal

propensity

See GCCISD Vocabulary Guide for activities and assessments. | Review cursive writing through daily writing instruction

Directly teach strokes, letter formation, and heading as needed.

Please Note:

80% of all written student work should be done in cursive.

See GCCISD Handwriting Guide for activities. | Review Report Form and Story Form.

See Story Form and Report Form Guide for activities and passages. | Weekly listening and speaking activities may include:

- Teacher-selected materials
- Journal responses
- Current events
- Oral presentations
- Listening activity tapes
(Learn to Listen) |
| Mock TAAS Objective Assessments based on calendar year | Mock TAAS Objective Assessments based on calendar year | Mock TAAS | Weekly Tests | Unit 5 Assessment | | | |

Language Arts Scope and Sequence
Grade 5 – Sixth Six Weeks

Reading	Grammar	Writing	Spelling	Vocabulary	Handwriting	Project Read	Listening/Speaking
Cover each TAAS objective according to campus calendar. Assessments will be given based on calendar as well.	**Parts of Speech** Prepositions Review Parts of Speech **Usage** Review and practice Usage rules using TAAS formatted pages and through composition writing. **Sentence Construction** Review and practice Sentence Construction using TAAS formatted pages and through composition writing.	**Daily Writing** - journals - story summaries - article reviews - etc. **TAAS Focus** Review all modes. **Research**	**Week 31 Skills** r-controlled letter pattern **Week 32 Skills** r-controlled letter pattern **Week 33 Skills** Diphthong letter patterns	Unit 1 absorbent affluent candor compress confusion drivel	Review cursive writing through daily writing instruction. Directly teach strokes, letter formation, and heading as needed.	Review Report Form and Story Form.	Weekly listening and speaking activities may include: - Teacher-selected materials - Journal responses - Current events - Oral presentations - Listening activity tapes (Learn to Listen)
Please Note: Teachers will listen to each student read orally 1-2 times weekly. This should be done as part of regular reading and classroom instruction.	**Capitalization** Review and practice Capitalization rules using TAAS formatted pages and through composition writing. **Punctuation** Review and practice Punctuation rules using TAAS formatted pages and through composition writing.	Weekly class discussion on current events, film reviews, campus happenings, etc. Research must be done during the year. You may choose which six-week period in which to complete task. Use GCCISD rubrics and organizers for scoring and planning writing.	**Week 34 Skills** eigh = /ŭ/ -old = /fl/ igh = /Œ/ -oll = /fl/ ind = /Œ/ **Week 35 Skills** **Week 36 Skills**	facilitate incarcerate instigate manipulate paradox pervade precedent profuse prosperous	Please Note: 80% of all written student work should be done in cursive.		
See attached chart for correlating TAAS targets and reading instruction.	**Written Expression** Review Written Expression through composition writing.	See GCCSD Research Guide for activities.	See GCCISD Spelling Guide for words and activities.	See GCCISD Vocabulary Guide for activities and assessments.	See GCCISD Handwriting Guide for activities.	See Story Form and Report Form Guide for activities and passages.	
TAAS Reading			Weekly Tests	Unit 6 Assessment			

Objectives

Grades 6-8

Goose Creek Consolidated Independent School District
Baytown, Texas

SECONDARY READING/LANGUAGE ARTS OBJECTIVES
SIXTH GRADE

STUDENTS WILL BE ABLE TO:

I. Use and locate information in a library.
    A. Access a card catalog and computer terminal to locate books.
    B. Identify various library sections.
    C. Find and use reference materials:
        a. Encyclopedia
        b. Dictionary
        c. Atlas
        d. Almanac
        e. Reader's Guide
        f. Periodicals
2. Write about personal experiences on a regular basis.
3. Apply correct English usage, grammar, and spelling skills as appropriate to their writing. Respond orally and in writing to what they read.
4. Investigate forms of factual writing.
5. Investigate the modes of writing using the writing process.
6. Exhibit expertise in recognition and comprehension of content-related and enrichment vocabulary lists.
7. Identify story elements in a literary selection.
    A. Identify, define, and analyze the elements of a novel, play, and non-fiction work.
    B. Develop critical-reading skills
        a. Main idea
        b. Cause/effect
        c. Flashback
        d. Inference Skills
        e. Fact/Opinion
        f. Prediction of outcomes
        g. See pictures of what is read
        h. Summarize
8. Identify and analyze the elements of a short story:
    A. Plot
    B. Characterization
    C. Setting
    D. Mood
    E. Author's point of view
    F. Author's purpose
    G. Theme
9. Recognize and develop an understanding of various forms of poetry and create original poetry.
10. Demonstrate effective listening and speaking skills.
11. Utilize a variety of methods for effective study habits.
    A. Skim, scan, SQR 3, take notes, K-W-L (know, what to learn, what was learned).
    B. Practice effective test-taking strategies.

SECONDARY READING/LANGUAGE ARTS OBJECTIVES
SEVENTH GRADE

STUDENTS WILL BE ABLE TO:

1. Demonstrate the use of complex sentence structure.

2. Write multi-paragraph compositions that demonstrate fluency and transition.

3. Demonstrate the ability to use multiple resources for the purpose of research.

4. Read, comprehend, and analyze a selection.

5. Demonstrate the ability to vary reading rate according to purpose.

6. Strengthen and enhance the following "fix up" strategies:
    a. Monitor their own reading
    b. Read at a rate that does not interfere with meaning
    c. See pictures of what is read
    d. Make predictions
    e. Reconstruct the story
    f. Summarize

7. Examine a piece of literature and relate what they have read to personal experiences.

8. Produce factual/technical writings.

9. Apply correct English usage, grammar, and spelling skills as appropriate to their writing.

10. Respond orally and in writing to what they read.

11. Use and apply study skills.

12. Produce all modes of writing and demonstrate expertise for the classificatory and persuasive modes, which present only one side of an issue.

13. Exhibit expertise in recognition and comprehension of a content-related vocabulary list.

14. Demonstrate effective listening and speaking skills.

SECONDARY READING/LANGUAGE ARTS OBJECTIVES
EIGHTH GRADE

STUDENTS WILL BE ABLE TO:

1. Demonstrate the use of complex sentence structure in all written work.

2. Maintain proficiency in well-elaborated compositions.

3. Complete a research project that reflects expertise in investigation skills.

4. Read, comprehend, evaluate, and analyze a selection.

5. Select appropriate reading rate according to purpose. Analyze and choose the appropriate "fix up" strategies from the following list:
   a. Monitor their own reading
   b. Read at a rate that does not interfere with meaning
   c. See pictures of what is read
   d. Make predictions
   e. Retell the story
   f. Summarize

6. Apply correct English usage, grammar, and spelling skills as appropriate to their writing.

7. Use and apply study skills to their own learning.

8. Exhibit expertise in recognition and comprehension of a content-related vocabulary list.

9. Demonstrate effective listening and speaking skills.

10. Create writing based on personal experiences.

11. Produce and evaluate factual/technical writings.

12. Respond orally and in writing to what they read.

13. Demonstrate proficiency in all modes of writing, emphasizing the production of papers, which include the discussion of two sides of an issue.

14. Exhibit the characteristics of an expert reader.

Reasonable Expectations

Language Arts
Enriched/GATE/Pre-AP

Grades 6-12

Draft

Goose Creek Consolidated Independent School District
Baytown, Texas

REASONABLE EXPECTATIONS

Minimum amount of work required by students each 6 weeks (both independent and class work)	Sixth Grade	Seventh Grade	Eighth Grade
Oral presentation	Twice a year (group or individual)	3 times a year	4 times a year
Grammar/usage/ language	Up to 40% of time spent direct-teaching grammar	Up to 30% of time spent direct-teaching grammar	Up to 25% of time spent direct-teaching grammar
Vocabulary	Minimum of 5 words per week appropriate to unit/needs of students; spelling may be part of vocabulary	Daily writing One good piece – one which must be a product of research	Daily writing One good piece – one which must be a product of research
Reading	4 books a year	5 books a year	5 books a year
Spelling	Up to 15 minutes a week direct-teaching spelling	Minimum of 5 words per week – appropriate to unit/needs of students	Minimum of 5 words per week – appropriate to unit/needs of students
Amount of time in library	Minimum 120 minutes per 6 weeks (library skills)	Minimum 120 minutes per 6 weeks (library skills)	Minimum 120 minutes per 6 weeks (library skills)
Writing	Writing responses to key pieces of literature 1. Frequent prompt-response writing 2. Writing process develops each mode	Writing response journal to key pieces of literature	Writing response journal to key pieces of literature
Daily Oral Reading	Daily reading – preferred 60 minutes of independent reading a week	Daily reading	Daily reading
	4 books a year	5 books a year	5 books a year

ENRICHED/GATE/PRE-AP
REASONABLE EXPECTATIONS

	SIXTH GRADE		SEVENTH GRADE		EIGHTH GRADE	
	ENRICHED	GATE/PRE-AP	ENRICHED	GATE/PRE-AP	ENRICHED	GATE/PRE-AP
VOCABULARY (per 6 weeks)	50	60	60	80	60-75	90-120
*WRITING ASSIGNMENTS (per year)	15	17	6	12	6	10
	Single paragraphs		Multi-paragraphs		Multi-paragraphs	
NUMBER OF BOOKS (in and out of class per year)	10	12	12	16	18	20
NUMBER OF PROJECTS (per year)	1	3	2	2	3	4
RESEARCH (per year)	Introduction to research		1 research paper	1 Major research paper	1 Major research paper / 3 Reports	1 Major research paper / 4 small reports
ORAL PRESENTATIONS (per year)	1	3	6	6	3	4
	Informal		Informal		Informal	

* The number of writing assignments decreases due to length, complexity of topic, elaboration, emphasis on reasoning and logic, etc

ENRICHED/GATE SIXTH-GRADE LANGUAGE ARTS

FIRST SIX WEEKS	SECOND SIX WEEKS	THIRD SIX WEEKS
Vocabulary – 50 words (compilation of words from lists, novels, and programs) Writing/grammar – In paragraph construction focus on topic sentence, supporting details, concluding sentence (at least 4 samples). Use mini-lessons, rubrics, and correction sheets to address grammar objectives. Research Literature/reading – minimum of 2 full-length selections, as well as selected short stories and non-fiction. Reading skills	Vocabulary – 50 words Writing/grammar – In narrative essay focus on three-part structure: introduction, body, and conclusion. Use writing process to complete 1 final draft. Use mini-lessons, rubrics, and correction sheets to address grammar objectives. Research Literature/reading	Vocabulary – 50 words Writing/grammar – In descriptive essay focus on sensory, spatial order, and specific word choice. Use mini-lessons, rubrics, and correction sheets to address grammar objectives. Research Literature/reading
FOURTH SIX WEEKS	**FIFTH SIX WEEKS**	**SIXTH SIX WEEKS**
Vocabulary – 50 words Writing/grammar – In how-to essay focus on structure and sequential order. Use writing process to complete final draft. Use mini-lessons, rubrics, and correction sheets to address grammar objectives. Research Literature/reading	Vocabulary – 50 words Writing/grammar – In comparison/contrast essay focus on structure and strong support. Use writing process to complete final draft. Use mini-lessons, rubrics, and correction sheets to address grammar objectives. Research Literature/reading	Vocabulary – 50 words Writing/grammar – In persuasion essay focus on ways to support: Quote from source, dialogue, anecdote, and survey statistics. Use mini-lessons, rubrics, and correction sheets to address grammar objectives. Research Literature/reading

- Research/reference materials – encyclopedia, dictionary, atlas, almanac, reader's guide, periodicals (focus on bibliography and note cards)
- Reading skills
- Literature/reading skills – plot/sequential order, setting, characterization, mood, point of view, theme/main idea, cause/effect, flashback, inference, fact/opinion, summarization, recognition of supporting facts/details, logical conclusion, predicting outcomes (foreshadowing), chart/graph interpretation, figurative language, conflict, symbolism, tone, connotation/denotation, other

ENRICHED/GATE SEVENTH GRADE LANGUAGE ARTS

FIRST SIX WEEKS	SECOND SIX WEEKS	THIRD SIX WEEKS
Vocabulary – 80 words TAAS (Texas Assessment of Academic Skills) writing – 2 persuasive essays (5 paragraphs minimum) Research Literature/reading (skills listed below – 3 full-length selections, selected short stories, non-fiction Grammar skills Oral presentations (6 per year)	Vocabulary – 80 words TAAS writing – 2 comparison/contrast essays (5 paragraphs minimum) Research Literature/reading (skills listed below) – 3 full-length selections selected short stories, non-fiction Grammar skills	Vocabulary – 80 words TAAS writing – 2 how-to essays (5 paragraphs minimum) Research Literature/reading (skills listed below) – 3 full-length selections, selected short stories, non-fiction Grammar skills
FOURTH SIX WEEKS	**FIFTH SIX WEEKS**	**SIXTH SIX WEEKS**
Vocabulary – 80 words TAAS writing – 2 descriptive essays (5 paragraphs minimum) Research Literature/reading (skills listed below) – 3 full-length selections, selected short stories, non-fiction Grammar skills	Vocabulary – 80 words TAAS writing – 2 essays reviewing all modes/narratives (5 paragraphs minimum) Research Literature/reading (skills listed below) – 3 full-length selections, selected short stories, non-fiction Grammar skills	Vocabulary – 80 words Writing – poetry/fantasy Research Literature/reading (skills listed below) – 3 full-length selections, selected short stories, non-fiction Grammar skills

- TAAS writing – must include pre-writing, rough draft, final draft, rubrics, correction sheet
- Vocabulary – compilation from novels, lists, programs
- Research – bibliography card for six different types of sources, internal footnotes, quote incorporation (reading-based)
- Literature/reading skills – plot/sequential order, setting, characterization, mood, point of view, theme/main idea, cause/effect, flashback, inference, fact/opinion, summarization, recognition of supporting facts/details, logical conclusion, predicting outcomes (foreshadowing), chart/graph interpretation, figurative language, conflict, symbolism, tone, connotation/denotation, other

SEVENTH-GRADE PRE-AP STYLISTIC ELEMENTS
REASONABLE EXPECTATIONS BY SIX-WEEK PERIODS

FIRST SIX WEEKS	SECOND SIX WEEKS	THIRD SIX WEEKS
AMOUNT AND TYPES OF READING	AMOUNT AND TYPES OF READING	AMOUNT AND TYPES OF READING
Outside reading – 1 full-length novel	Outside reading – 1 full-length novel	Outside reading – 1 full-length novel
Teacher-directed – 1 novel at least (100-200 pages)	Teacher-directed – 1 novel at least (100-200 pages)	Teacher-directed – 1 novel at least (100-200 pages)
Figurative language (simile, metaphor, personification)	Figurative language (simile, metaphor, personification)	Figurative language (simile, metaphor, personification)
Supplemented by short stories, poetry, or non-fiction	Supplemented by short stories, poetry, or non-fiction	Supplemented by short stories, poetry, or non-fiction
Oral presentation – once per 6 weeks	Oral presentation – once per 6 weeks	Oral presentation – once per 6 weeks
Grammar, usage, language – no more than 30% of time spent direct-teaching	Grammar, usage, language – no more than 30% of time spent direct-teaching	Grammar, usage, language – no more than 30% of time spent direct-teaching
AMOUNT AND TYPES OF WRITING	Connotation vs. denotation and point of view	Connotation vs. denotation and point of view
Daily writing	AMOUNT AND TYPES OF WRITING	Personification
1 good piece of TAAS (Texas Assessment of Academic Skills) writing	Daily writing	AMOUNT AND TYPES OF WRITING
Enriched/GATE already do more than regular classes – Science Fair, History Fair, and 1 in English with footnotes, bibliography, etc.	1 good piece of TAAS writing	Daily writing
	1 research paper for the year	1 good piece of TAAS writing
	AMOUNT AND TYPES OF VOCABULARY	1 research paper for the year
AMOUNT AND TYPES OF VOCABULARY		1 timed (40 minutes) writing in the AP essay format
	Minimum 10 words per week vocabulary workshop from Sadlier-Oxford	AMOUNT AND TYPES OF VOCABULARY
Minimum 10 words per week vocabulary workshop from Sadlier-Oxford		Minimum 10 words per week vocabulary workshop from Sadlier-Oxford

SEVENTH GRADE PRE-AP STYLISTIC ELEMENTS
REASONABLE EXPECTATIONS BY SIX-WEEK PERIODS

FOURTH SIX WEEKS	FIFTH SIX WEEKS	SIXTH SIX WEEKS
AMOUNT AND TYPES OF READING	AMOUNT AND TYPES OF READING	AMOUNT AND TYPES OF READING
Outside reading – 1 full-length novel	Outside reading – 1 full-length novel	Outside reading – 1 full-length novel
Teacher-directed – 1 novel at least (100-200 pages)	Teacher-directed – 1 novel at least (100-200 pages)	Teacher-directed – 1 novel at least (100-200 pages)
Figurative language (simile, metaphor)	Figurative language (simile, metaphor)	Figurative language (simile, metaphor)
Supplemented by short stories, poetry, or non-fiction	Supplemented by short stories, poetry, or non-fiction	Supplemented by short stories, poetry, or non-fiction
Oral presentation – once per 6 weeks	Oral presentation – once per 6 weeks	Oral presentation – once per 6 weeks
Grammar, usage, language – no more than 30% of time spent direct-teaching	Grammar, usage, language – no more than 30% of time spent direct-teaching	Grammar, usage, language – no more than 30% of time spent direct-teaching
Refining stylistic elements introduced first semester (more in-depth)	Connotation vs. denotation and point of view	Connotation vs. denotation and point of view
AMOUNT AND TYPES OF WRITING	AMOUNT AND TYPES OF WRITING	AMOUNT AND TYPES OF WRITING
1 timed writing (40 minutes) in the AP essay format	Daily writing	Daily writing
Test writing in the AP format (3 total for the year)	1 good piece of TAAS writing	1 good piece of TAAS writing
AMOUNT AND TYPES OF VOCABULARY	1 research paper for the year	1 research paper for the year
Minimum 10 words per week vocabulary workshop from Sadlier-Oxford	AMOUNT AND TYPES OF VOCABULARY	1 timed (40 minutes) writing in the AP essay format
	Minimum 10 words per week vocabulary workshop from Sadlier-Oxford	AMOUNT AND TYPES OF VOCABULARY
		Minimum 10 words per week vocabulary workshop from Sadlier-Oxford

REASONABLE EXPECTATIONS
EIGHTH-GRADE LANGUAGE ARTS

ENRICHED	GATE
5 novels/full-length works	10-15 novels/full-length works (teacher guided; used for in-class instruction)
10-12 short stories	10-15 short stories
13 independent readings	10 independent readings
5 major papers incorporating all stages of writing process (1 per 6 weeks)	1-2 major papers each 6 weeks incorporating all stages of writing process
1 major research paper done independently or in conjunction with history fair or science fair	1 major research paper done independently or in conjunction with history fair or science fair

Daily writings
    Journals
    Prompts
    Response guides
	Daily writings
	    Journals
	    Prompts
	    Response guides

10-15 vocabulary words weekly	15-20 vocabulary words weekly
3 oral presentations	4 oral presentations
3 projects	4 projects
	4 minor research assignments

EIGHTH-GRADE
PRE-AP ENGLISH/GATE COURSE DESCRIPTION AND EXPECTATIONS

Statement of Philosophy: This class is designed for college bound students who desire a rigorous, advanced-level class.

CLASS REQUIREMENTS	CLASS FOCUS
Vocabulary words – 5-10 used in meaningful sentences a week	Analysis and criticism of literary artifacts will be studied.
Timed writings – at least 1 45-minute writing per week	Discussion will focus on identified eighth-grade Pre-AP skills, which include but are not limited to imagery, diction, and author's purpose/attitude. Other skills practiced include archetypes, satire, symbolism, irony, mood, tone, theme, and figurative language.
Daily journal writing – center on literary analysis and criticism	
Reading – 12 novels total per year (equivalent to 70-80 pages per week)	Basic argumentation, which centers on development of assertions supported by evidence and proven using commentary, will be practiced.

Projects – up to 6 per year
   Projects may be in following forms:
   * written   * research-based
   * dramatic   * reading study guides
   * oral   * artistic
	Developing successful study habits is necessary.

Research papers – up to 2: *1 in conjunction with history fair *1 independent	
TAAS (Texas Assessment of Academic Skills) writings – 5-10 per year	
Major test – at conclusion of in-class novels or as material warrants: * styled after AP test * may include essay prompt(s) and/or multiple-choice questions	
Study time – if study time exceeds 1½ hours per night, please notify teacher	

EIGHTH-GRADE PRE-AP
ENRICHED ENGLISH COURSE DESCRIPTION AND EXPECTATIONS

Statement of Philosophy: This class is designed for college-bound students who desire an advanced-level class.

CLASS REQUIREMENTS	CLASS FOCUS

Vocabulary words – 5-10 used meaningfully
 	
Timed writings – up to 2 per 6 weeks
 	
Daily journal writing – center on guided and independent response journals
 	
Reading – 12 novels total per year (equivalent to 70-80 pages per week)
 	
Projects – up to 6 per year
    Projects may be in following forms:
    * written   * research-based
    * dramatic   * reading study guides
    * oral   * artistic
 	
Research papers – up to 2:
*1 in conjunction with history fair
* several shorter research projects or papers
 	
TAAS (Texas Assessment of Academic Skills) writings – 5 per year, using all stages of writing process
 	
Major test – at conclusion of in-class novels or as material warrants:
* resembling AP-type questions
* may include essay prompt(s) and/or multiple-choice questions
 	
Study time – if study time exceeds 1½ hours per night, please notify teacher
	Analysis and criticism of literary artifacts will be studied.
	
	Discussion will focus on identified eighth-grade Pre-AP skills, which include but are not limited to imagery, diction, and author's purpose/attitude. Other skills practiced include archetypes, satire, symbolism, irony, mood, tone, theme, and figurative language.
	
	Basic argumentation, which centers on development of assertions supported by evidence and proven using commentary, will be practiced.
	
	Developing successful study habits is necessary.

EIGHTH-GRADE PRE-AP/GATE SKILLS:
IMAGERY, DICTION, AUTHOR'S POINT OF VIEW/ATTITUDE
REASONABLE EXPECTATIONS BY SIX-WEEK PERIODS

FIRST SIX WEEKS	SECOND SIX WEEKS	THIRD SIX WEEKS
AMOUNT AND TYPES OF READING 1 full-length novel AMOUNT AND TYPES OF WRITING 1 TAAS (Texas Assessment of Academic Skills) paper, research, or literary Daily writing (journals, responses, analysis, critiques, etc.) AMOUNT AND TYPES OF VOCABULARY 5-10 words per week/SAT words; literary terms to be used in meaningful context	AMOUNT AND TYPES OF READING 1 full-length novel 1 independent novel AMOUNT AND TYPES OF WRITING 1 TAAS paper, research, or literary Daily writing AMOUNT AND TYPES OF VOCABULARY 5-10 words per week/SAT words; literary terms to be used in meaningful context	AMOUNT AND TYPES OF READING 1 full-length novel 1 independent novel AMOUNT AND TYPES OF WRITING 1 TAAS paper, research, or literary Daily writing AMOUNT AND TYPES OF VOCABULARY 5-10 words per week/SAT words; literary terms to be used in meaningful context
FOURTH SIX WEEKS	**FIFTH SIX WEEKS**	**SIXTH SIX WEEKS**
AMOUNT AND TYPES OF READING AMOUNT AND TYPES OF WRITING 1 TAAS paper, research, or literary AMOUNT AND TYPES OF VOCABULARY 5-10 words per week/SAT words; literary terms to be used in meaningful context	AMOUNT AND TYPES OF READING AMOUNT AND TYPES OF WRITING 1 TAAS paper, research, or literary AMOUNT AND TYPES OF VOCABULARY 5-10 words per week/SAT words; literary terms to be used in meaningful context	AMOUNT AND TYPES OF READING AMOUNT AND TYPES OF WRITING 1 TAAS paper, research, or literary AMOUNT AND TYPES OF VOCABULARY 5-10 words per week/SAT words; literary terms to be used in meaningful context

* All 5 TAAS purposes/modes are required by the end of the year.

NINTH-GRADE PRE-AP
REASONABLE EXPECTATIONS BY SIX-WEEK PERIODS

FIRST SIX WEEKS	SECOND SIX WEEKS	THIRD SIX WEEKS
AMOUNT AND TYPES OF READING Short story (based on elements of short story) Minimum of 1 story per element (4-6) Outside reading (1-2 novels) – teacher discretion AMOUNT AND TYPES OF WRITING Narrative, character sketch, descriptive AMOUNT AND TYPES OF VOCABULARY Literary terms (by example); 35 words (approximately) related to short story	AMOUNT AND TYPES OF READING Epic poem/novel; 1-3 novels – teacher discretion Outside reading (1-2 novels) AMOUNT AND TYPES OF WRITING Epic-journey persuasive, Pre-AP timed writing – choice Outside reading AMOUNT AND TYPES OF VOCABULARY 30 SAT words Vocabulary terms associated with literary selections Literary terms	AMOUNT AND TYPES OF READING *Great Expectations*/alternate novel 1-3 novels – teacher discretion Outside reading AMOUNT AND TYPES OF WRITING Expository, Pre-AP timed writing AMOUNT AND TYPES OF VOCABULARY 30 SAT words Literary terms Terms associated with literary selections
FOURTH SIX WEEKS	**FIFTH SIX WEEKS**	**SIXTH SIX WEEKS**
AMOUNT AND TYPES OF READING Poetry, drama – *Romeo and Juliet*/alternate selection 1-3 novels – teacher discretion Outside reading AMOUNT AND TYPES OF WRITING Comparison/contrast Imagery analysis Pre-AP timed writing AMOUNT AND TYPES OF VOCABULARY Literary terms (poetry) 10 SAT words Terms associated with literary selections	AMOUNT AND TYPES OF READING Novel/review for Pre-AP 1-3 novels – teacher discretion Outside reading AMOUNT AND TYPES OF WRITING Literary analysis (prep for Pre-AP) Pre-AP timed writing AMOUNT AND TYPES OF VOCABULARY Pre-AP words review 10 SAT words Literary terms Terms associated with literary selections	AMOUNT AND TYPES OF READING Novel 1-3 novels – teacher discretion Outside reading AMOUNT AND TYPES OF WRITING 1 TAAS (Texas Assessment of Academic Skills) review (persuasion) AMOUNT AND TYPES OF VOCABULARY 30 SAT words Literary terms Terms associated with literary selections

TENTH-GRADE PRE-AP/GATE ELEMENTS
LITERARY TERMS, POINT OF VIEW, PERSUASIVE WRITING, TIMED WRITINGS
REASONABLE EXPECTATIONS BY SIX-WEEK PERIODS

FIRST SIX WEEKS	SECOND SIX WEEKS	THIRD SIX WEEKS
AMOUNT AND TYPES OF READING Outside reading/1 work of fiction AMOUNT AND TYPES OF WRITING 1 expository piece 2 descriptive paragraphs Journal/portfolio (minimum of 2 entries) AMOUNT AND TYPES OF VOCABULARY 10 words per week/SAT words	AMOUNT AND TYPES OF READING Short stories minimum of 3, maximum of 12 Outside reading – 1 work of fiction AMOUNT AND TYPES OF WRITING 1 research paper Timed writing Journal/portfolio (minimum of 1 entry) AMOUNT AND TYPES OF VOCABULARY 10 words per week/SAT words	AMOUNT AND TYPES OF READING *Legends of King Arthur* (3 selections) *Camelot/A Connecticut Yankee in King Arthur's Court* 1 TAAS (Texas Assessment of Academic Skills) practice essay AMOUNT AND TYPES OF WRITING Journal/portfolio (minimum of 1 entry) AMOUNT AND TYPES OF VOCABULARY 10 words per week/SAT words
FOURTH SIX WEEKS	**FIFTH SIX WEEKS**	**SIXTH SIX WEEKS**
AMOUNT AND TYPES OF READING TAAS Poetry Outside reading – 1 non-fiction, 1 biography AMOUNT AND TYPES OF WRITING TAAS Poetry (1 free-verse poem containing figurative language) AMOUNT AND TYPES OF VOCABULARY 10 words per week/SAT words	AMOUNT AND TYPES OF READING *Julius Caesar/Midsummer Night's Dream* or *Twelve Angry Men*/drama Outside reading – student selection AMOUNT AND TYPES OF WRITING Timed writing Journal/portfolio (1 entry) AMOUNT AND TYPES OF VOCABULARY 10 words per week/SAT words	AMOUNT AND TYPES OF READING *A Separate Peace*/novel limit Outside reading – student selection AMOUNT AND TYPES OF WRITING Timed writing Journal/portfolio (1 entry) AMOUNT AND TYPES OF VOCABULARY 10 words per week/SAT words

ELEVENTH-GRADE PRE-AP
REASONABLE EXPECTATIONS BY SIX-WEEK PERIODS

FIRST SIX WEEKS	SECOND SIX WEEKS	THIRD SIX WEEKS
AMOUNT AND TYPES OF READING Summer reading of 4 novels AMOUNT AND TYPES OF WRITING Reader's journals covering all summer reading Option for open prompts for all or part of summer readings Timed writing AMOUNT AND TYPES OF VOCABULARY Literary vocabulary District vocabulary	AMOUNT AND TYPES OF READING 3-5 long works, including plays of choice from American Literature Reading multiple non-fiction entries from modern and pre-19th-century literature AMOUNT AND TYPES OF WRITING Timed essays for all writing assignments AMOUNT AND TYPES OF VOCABULARY Literary and rhetorical vocabulary District vocabulary	AMOUNT AND TYPES OF READING 3-5 long works, including plays of choice from American Literature Reading multiple non-fiction entries from modern and pre-19th-century literature AMOUNT AND TYPES OF WRITING Timed essays for all writing assignments AMOUNT AND TYPES OF VOCABULARY Literary and rhetorical vocabulary District vocabulary
FOURTH SIX WEEKS	**FIFTH SIX WEEKS**	**SIXTH SIX WEEKS**
AMOUNT AND TYPES OF READING Literary research paper Novelists and 2-3 works to be completed by end of 6 weeks AMOUNT AND TYPES OF WRITING Argumentation/deconstruction, construction Poetry (1 free-verse poem containing figurative language) AMOUNT AND TYPES OF VOCABULARY Literary vocabulary District vocabulary	AMOUNT AND TYPES OF READING Dictionary of Literary Biography, contemporary literary criticism, critical materials, and reread sections of novels from fourth six weeks AMOUNT AND TYPES OF WRITING Literary research paper AMOUNT AND TYPES OF VOCABULARY Literary vocabulary District vocabulary	AMOUNT AND TYPES OF READING In-class novel and out-of-class work Non-fiction selection Reading-comprehension materials AMOUNT AND TYPES OF WRITING Language and comprehension magazine Writing exam AMOUNT AND TYPES OF VOCABULARY Literary vocabulary District vocabulary

TWELFTH-GRADE PRE-AP
REASONABLE EXPECTATIONS BY SIX-WEEK PERIODS

FIRST SIX WEEKS	SECOND SIX WEEKS	THIRD SIX WEEKS
AMOUNT AND TYPES OF READING 7 outside readings (of literary merit) 7 in-class readings (of literary merit); teacher conference 1 novel – assigned AMOUNT AND TYPES OF WRITING Creative essay – *Beowulf* Personal essay College prompt AMOUNT AND TYPES OF VOCABULARY Literary terms – 10 (in context)	AMOUNT AND TYPES OF READING Novel (assigned or student choice) AMOUNT AND TYPES OF WRITING Characterization: hero, personality Practice of prompts (timed writing) AMOUNT AND TYPES OF VOCABULARY Literary terms – 1 (in context)	AMOUNT AND TYPES OF READING Novel (assigned or student choice) AMOUNT AND TYPES OF WRITING AP prompts (impromptu), based on literature Motifs in *Macbeth* AMOUNT AND TYPES OF VOCABULARY Literary terms – 1 (in context)
FOURTH SIX WEEKS	**FIFTH SIX WEEKS**	**SIXTH SIX WEEKS**
AMOUNT AND TYPES OF READING Novel (assigned or student choice) AMOUNT AND TYPES OF WRITING Research paper AMOUNT AND TYPES OF VOCABULARY Literary terms – research-related	AMOUNT AND TYPES OF READING Novel (assigned or student choice) AMOUNT AND TYPES OF WRITING Explication of poetry Allegory AP prompts (timed writing) AMOUNT AND TYPES OF VOCABULARY Literary terms	AMOUNT AND TYPES OF READING Comedy and/or short stories Drama AMOUNT AND TYPES OF WRITING Personal AMOUNT AND TYPES OF VOCABULARY Literary terms

Process 3: Measuring Student Growth

Growth is measured against standards of performance (not grades). Examples of tools used to measure growth include Benchmarks, Rubrics, and Ten-Question Tests. Use these tools to find students who are having trouble.

Knowing who is in trouble
    Enables us to select the best intervention and
        Implement it in a targeted fashion
            For the greatest impact.

BENCHMARKS

A benchmark is a simple model listing three or four indicators by grading period to show whether a student needs an immediate intervention. See full explanation in Appendix, Campuswide Interventions That Improve Student Achievement, ***Instructional Leader***, November 1996.

RUBRICS

A rubric provides a means of showing growth against a standard instead of just giving a grade. A good rubric looks at characteristics of skilled learners within a subject area. For example: a skilled reader – fluent, motivated, makes meaning, able to predict, strategic readers. For those characteristics …

1. Identify criteria to be assessed.
2. Identify what a 4 (best) would be and what a 1 (worst) would be.
3. Identify markers for a 2 and a 3.

One easy way to use a rubric is to highlight the phrases that describe a student's work for the file or to show a parent, then use a different color to highlight the student's work in the next marking period. It easily demonstrates progress between assessments.

See reading and math rubrics included in this manual.

TEN-QUESTION TESTS

The faculty or a group of teachers gets together and writes 10 questions in the subject area that reflect the standards taught; all teachers in the subject area or course include these on the six-or nine-week test.

Benchmarks

**Developed by the Faculty of
Runyan Elementary, Grades 1-4
Conroe, Texas**

Principal: Nancy Harris

KINDERGARTEN BENCHMARKS

FIRST SIX WEEKS	SECOND SIX WEEKS
Journal Writing	**Journal Writing**
Draw a picture that tells a story – dictate	Draw a picture
Know rules for using writing materials: pencils, markers, gluing, scissors	Attempt controlled, scribbled-letter approximation
Use rules	Use letter strings
THIRD SIX WEEKS	**FOURTH SIX WEEKS**
Journal Writing	**Journal Writing**
Draw a picture	Draw a picture
Attempt to write beginning sounds	Attempt to use descriptive words
Write using invented (developmental) spelling	Write using developmental spelling
Write first name	
FIFTH SIX WEEKS	**SIXTH SIX WEEKS**
Journal Writing	**Journal Writing**
Write using developmental spelling	Write first and last name
	Write using developmental spelling

FIRST-GRADE READING BENCHMARKS

FIRST SIX WEEKS

Write first name legibly

Left-to-right and return sweep (sweep
    directionality)

One-to-one matching

Identify name and main sound for consonant
    letters

Predict meaning from picture clues

SECOND SIX WEEKS

Read Level 6 book with 90% accuracy,
    including good fluency

Identify beginning, middle, and end of story
    (early story structure)

Identify correct sentence structure
    (begins with capital, ends with
    punctuation)

Identify beginning and ending sounds of words

Identify differences among letters, words,
    sentences

THIRD SIX WEEKS

Read Level 9 book with 90% accuracy,
    including good fluency

Identify short vowels in words in reading

Use phrasing and punctuation in oral reading

FOURTH SIX WEEKS

Read Level 12 book with 90% accuracy
    including good fluency

Use self-extending system
    (Reading Recovery Guidebook)
    (7 strategies to use while reading)

Identify main characters

FIFTH SIX WEEKS

Read Level 15 book with 90% accuracy
    including good fluency

Use self-extending system

Identify cause and effect in story

Retell orally and in writing a story read by
    teacher and/or independently

Identify story problem

SIXTH SIX WEEKS

Read Level 16 book with 90% accuracy,
    including good fluency

Be able to differentiate between non-fiction
    and fiction

Use self-extending system

Choose appropriate books for independent
    reading

FIRST-GRADE MATH BENCHMARKS

FIRST SEMESTER	SECOND SEMESTER
Conserve numbers to 8	Write numbers to 50
More/less	Add and subtract numbers without regrouping
One-to-one correspondence	Place value of 1's and 10's
	Addition facts to 10
	Subtraction facts to 10
	Conserve numbers to 10
	Steps to decide which operation in (+) or (-) is needed

SECOND-GRADE READING BENCHMARKS

FIRST SIX WEEKS

90% accuracy at reading Level 16

Make prediction using picture clues

Identify characters

Distinguish between fiction and non-fiction

Write 2-3 sentences on same topic using correct capitalization, punctuation, and spacing between words (personal narrative)

SECOND SIX WEEKS

90% accuracy at Level 17

Identify setting

Identify beginning, middle, and ending of story

Write how-to using 6-7 lines on same subject

THIRD SIX WEEKS

Identify main idea

Sequence order of 8-10 events

Write how-to using minimum of 5-7 steps in paragraph form

FOURTH SIX WEEKS

90% accuracy at Level 18

Prepare list of descriptives – same subject

FIFTH SIX WEEKS

90% accuracy at Level 19

Distinguish between main idea and details

Write descriptive narrative using 7 sentences on same subject

SIXTH SIX WEEKS

90% accuracy at Level 20

Distinguish among how-to, descriptive narrative, and personal narrative

Write comparison/contrast essay using 1 sentence to state subject, 3 sentences same, 3 sentences different

70% accuracy in use of capitalization, ending punctuation, spelling of high-frequency words

SECOND-GRADE MATH BENCHMARKS

FIRST SEMESTER

Order numbers least to greatest and greatest to least

Distinguish before, after, between

Know and use problem-solving process

Basic fact families (1-10) – memorize

Place value of 1's, 10's, 100's – read/write

Add with and without regrouping 2- and 3-digit numbers

SECOND SEMESTER

Subtract with and without regrouping 2- and 3-digit numbers

Tell time to hour, ½ hour, ¼ hour

Money – value of all coins
  Add and subtract coins

Name, identify, compare fractional parts

Recognize solids, congruency, symmetry

THIRD-GRADE LANGUAGE ARTS BENCHMARKS

FIRST SIX WEEKS

Use contextual clues to determine meaning of unfamiliar word

Recognize common relationship words that affect sentence meaning

Develop story map independently

Generate ideas using variety of strategies (brainstorming, webbing)

Recognize and produce complete sentences

SECOND SIX WEEKS

Use contextual clues to draw conclusions and make predictions

Write concise summarization of story/article in 3-5 sentences

Use descriptive language

Read with 90% accuracy at 3.3 level for fiction, 2.8 for non-fiction

Develop conferencing skills

THIRD SIX WEEKS

In written form, explain steps in how to do something

Develop editing skills

Share products of composition in variety of ways

Infer and generalize from written text

Read with 90% accuracy at 3.5 level for fiction, 3.0 for non-fiction

FOURTH SIX WEEKS

Group related sentences into paragraphs

Develop meaning by using cause and effect

Read with 90% accuracy at 3.7 level for fiction, 3.2 for non-fiction

Evaluate test using fact and opinion

Recall facts and data from written form

FIFTH SIX WEEKS

Recognize author's technique and point of view

Read with 90% accuracy at 3.9 level for fiction, 3.3 for non-fiction

Find main idea in written text

Recognize persuasive technique

Draw conclusions from written text

SIXTH SIX WEEKS

Develop note-taking strategies

Read with 90% accuracy at 4.0 level for fiction, 3.4 for non-fiction

THIRD-GRADE MATH BENCHMARKS

FIRST SIX WEEKS

Solve problem(s) using 4-5 steps with symbols

Read and write 4-digit numbers

Compare and order numbers

Add and subtract 3 digits with trades

Explain math problem with visual and/or written text

SECOND SIX WEEKS

Demonstrate understanding of multiplication

Add and subtract 4-digit numbers with trades

Determine which customary measurement to use

Add columns of 2- to 3-digit numbers

Round numbers to nearest 10 and 100

Estimate customary measurement

THIRD SIX WEEKS

Master multiplication facts

Identify fractional part of whole and fractional part of set

Determine which metric measurement to use

Interpret data to solve problems

Know and use different functions of calculator

FOURTH SIX WEEKS

Determine elapsed time

Identify, add, subtract, and estimate money

Determine which operation to use in word problem (+, -, x)

Identify decimals in 10^{ths} and 100^{ths}

FIFTH SIX WEEKS

Identify plane and space figures

Find perimeter, area, and volume

Understand parallel lines, intersecting lines, angles, segments, and points

Understand congruency

Understand relationship between fractions and probability

SIXTH SIX WEEKS

Read and interpret statistical data

Understand ordered pairs and plot grids

Demonstrate understanding of division concept

FOURTH-GRADE LANGUAGE ARTS BENCHMARKS

FIRST SIX WEEKS

Edit fragments and run-ons in own writing

Identify and define figurative and literal meaning

Write organized, elaborated descriptive paper

Be able to choose just-right books

SECOND SIX WEEKS

Identify story structure, orally and in written form

Write organized, elaborated expressive narrative

Identify correct subject/verb agreement and use in everyday writing

Use correct forms of pronouns in everyday writing

THIRD SIX WEEKS

Read passage and use contextual clues to decode unknown words

Read passage and recall facts and details orally and in writing

Read story or paragraph and sequence major events

Write organized, elaborated how-to

FOURTH SIX WEEKS

Read passage and identify main idea, orally and in written summary

Read passage and paraphrase in writing and orally

Write organized, elaborated classificatory paper

Read passage and identify best summary

Write 3- to 4-sentence paragraph

FIFTH SIX WEEKS

Use graphic sources to answer questions

Read passage to predict outcomes and draw conclusions

Distinguish between fact and non-fact, between stated and non-stated opinion

After reading passage, be able to tell cause of event or effect of action

Write organized, elaborated persuasive paper

SIXTH SIX WEEKS

Write assessment of chosen portfolio pieces

Assemble/share reading and writing portfolio

FOURTH-GRADE MATH BENCHMARKS

FIRST SIX WEEKS

Use list, graph, or table to interpret problem, and communicate solution in writing and orally

Use the four basic operations: add and subtract 3 digits, multiply and divide 3 digits by 1 digit

Sort and classify objects and numbers to demonstrate logical connections

Read and write numbers to 1 million

Use objects to compare fractions and determine equivalence

SECOND SIX WEEKS

Add and subtract with trades, including 0's and 4-digit mastery

Round up 4-digit numbers to nearest 10,000 and 1,000, including money

Compare and order 6-digit numbers from least to greatest and from greatest to least

Be able to choose appropriate unit of measurement to nearest inch, foot, yard, pound, and ounce in content problem

Be able to choose correct + or − operation to solve problem

THIRD SIX WEEKS

Evaluate reasonableness of an answer

Explain relationship between standard units of measurement

FOURTH SIX WEEKS

Be able to identify fraction that represents shaded and unshaded pictures

Determine perimeter in problems

Apply estimation and measurement of weight, length and capacity in metric and U.S. units

FIFTH SIX WEEKS

Tell time to nearest minute and solve problems using time duration

Predict, justify, and present rules for patterns to solve problems

Collect and organize data to create tables, Graphs, and charts

Justify, interpret, and communicate insightful conclusions from data

SIXTH SIX WEEKS

Create simple probability experiments

Use calculator to check predictions and computer solutions to problems.

Use computer software to display data, represent spatial relationships, and develop mathematical understanding to solve problems

FIFTH GRADE LANGUAGE ARTS BENCHMARKS

FIRST SIX WEEKS

Read grade-level fiction, non-fiction, poetry, and drama – recognize universal themes

Apply and articulate variety of comprehension strategies

Gain meaning of new vocabulary words in reading passages using context clues, diagrams, glossary, dictionary, thesaurus

SECOND SIX WEEKS

Develop awareness of how perspective and purpose define or influence form of media (i.e. point of view, bias, information, persuasion, entertainment, sensationalism, and personal testimony)

Read and interpret the following: written directions, diagrams, maps, charts, graphs, and tables

THIRD SIX WEEKS

Locate, collect, and utilize information from various sources: card catalog/computer system, computer/technology, encyclopedia, almanac, glossary, newspaper, atlas, thesaurus, index, dictionary

Apply writing process – prewriting, writing, revising/conferencing, rewriting/editing, publishing

Use writing process to improve word choice and conventions, especially sentence variety, capitalizing, punctuating, spelling, legible handwriting, and usage

FOURTH SIX WEEKS

Use writing process to organize writing, especially beginnings, middles and ends, using appropriate transitions

Recognize and apply the six traits of writing: ideas, content, organization, voice, word choice, sentence fluency

Recognize and apply various types of writing: journals, narrative, sequential, descriptive, research/report, compare/contrast, cause/effect, poetry, letters, outline/note-taking, persuasion, and short stories

Use word processing to publish a piece of writing

FIFTH SIX WEEKS

Select multimedia tool to enhance oral presentation

Present organized formal presentation on topic of personal interest or unit of study

Demonstrate listening comprehension by following oral directions and applying information to assigned tasks

SIXTH SIX WEEKS

Provide relevant feedback to speaker in form of question, comment, or elaboration

Interpret oral presentations using listening comprehension strategies

Integrate reading, writing, speaking, and listening skills into all content areas and personal life/goals

Use library skills and multi-media tools to access information and enhance presentations in all content areas and for variety of purposes

Adapted from: http://www.laramie1.k12.wy.us/instruction/langarts/benchmarklangart.htm

FIFTH GRADE MATH BENCHMARKS

FIRST SIX WEEKS

Apply math skills/mental math, number sense, estimation, rounding, and basic operations to solve problems

Choose strategy, apply deductive/inductive reasoning, and communicate process

Convert between common decimals, fractions, mixed numbers, percentages, and mixed numbers to improper fractions

SECOND SIX WEEKS

Add, subtract, and multiply 4-digit whole numbers and decimal numbers and divide whole/decimal numbers by single digit numbers

Find factors/multiples of whole numbers and recognize and represent integers (positive and negative)

Reduce any fraction whose Greatest Common Factor is 2-10, add/subtract like denominator fractions (12 or less), multiply fractions with denominators (10 or less) and divide whole numbers by unit fractions

THIRD SIX WEEKS

Use parentheses to order operations

Order/compare whole numbers through thousands, decimal numbers through thousandths, and fractions with like denominators (16 or less)

Recognize lines, rays, perpendicular/parallel lines, segments

FOURTH SIX WEEKS

Find perimeter using diagram or formula and use manipulatives to find areas of squares/rectangles

Make conjectures about congruence and similarity

Use geometric formulas

Solve real-world problems using time

FIFTH SIX WEEKS

Apply estimation/measurement of weight/mass, length, capacity in metric/U.S., and demonstrate relationship between metric/U.S. units

Determine, by counting, value of collection of coins, bills, and counting-back change from $1

Identify variables and translate phrases into numerical expressions

SIXTH SIX WEEKS

Plot points in quadrant 1 or on whole number line

Recognize, describe, extend, create, and generalize patterns

Collect, organize, and analyze data using tables, charts and graphs

Create probability experiments and make predictions

Adapted from: www.laramie1.k12.wy.us/instruction/math/benchmarkmath.htm

Reading Rubrics

Developed by the Faculty of Goose Creek Consolidated Independent School District Baytown, Texas

Reading Rubric, Grade 1

Student Name: _____   School Year: _____

Campus: _____   Grade: _____

	Beginning	Developing	Capable	Expert
Fluent	Decodes words haltingly	Decodes sentences haltingly	Knows vowel teams (ea, ee, oa, etc.)	Decodes polysyllabic words
	Misses key sounds	Knows conditions for long vowels (vowel at end of syllable, e.g., me, he)	Identifies common spelling patterns	Decodes words in context of paragraph
	Identifies most letter sounds	Identifies blends and consonants	Uses word-attack skills to identify new words	Decodes words accurately and automatically
	Identifies short vowels	Decodes digraphs and r-controlled vowels (or, ar, er, etc.)	Reads sentences in meaningful sequence	Reads paragraphs in meaningful sequence
	Says/recognizes individual words	Reads at rate that does not interfere with meaning	Reads with expression	Reads with expression, fluency, appropriate tone, and pronunciation
Constructive	Predictions are incomplete, partial, and unrelated	Predicts what might happen next	Predicts story based upon pictures and other clues	Can predict possible endings to story with some accuracy
	Predictions indicate no or inappropriate prior knowledge	Makes minimal links to personal experience/prior knowledge	Relates story to personal experience/prior knowledge	Can compare/ contrast story with personal experience
Motivated	Does not read independently	Reads when teacher or parent requests	Will read for specific purpose	Self-initiates reading
	Concentrates on decoding	Is eager to utilize acquired skills (words and phrases)	Uses new skills frequently in self-selected reading	Reads for pleasure

Strategic	Does not self-correct	Recognizes mistakes but has difficulty in self-correcting	Has strategies for self-correction (reread, read ahead, ask questions, etc.)	Analyzes self-correction strategies as to best strategy
	Is uncertain as to how parts of story fit together	Can identify characters and setting in story	Can identify characters, settings, and events of story	Can talk about · story in terms of problem and/or goal
Process	Cannot tell what has been read	Does not sort important from unimportant	Can determine with assistance what is important and unimportant	Organizes reading by sorting important from unimportant

Reading Rubric, Grade 2

Student Name: _____   School Year: _____

Campus: _____   Grade: _____

	Beginning	Developing	Capable	Expert
Fluent	Misses key phonemic elements	Knows basic phonetic structure of vowels: short, long, r-controlled, vowel teams	Uses word-attack skills to identify new words in section	Decoding not an issue; it is taken for granted
	Rate of reading interferes with meaning	Occasionally rate of reading interferes with meaning	Says sentences in meaningful sequence	Analyzes selection and uses most effective reading rate
	New vocabulary impairs understanding	Mispronounces unfamiliar words	Uses contextual clues to determine pronunciation of new words	Enjoys new words and practices using them in his/her vocabulary
Constructive	Makes some use of clues to determine what text will be about	Can predict what character might do next	Can predict possible outcomes from selection	Connects personal experience to predict outcomes
	May mention character he/she read about previously	Remembers general characters but not detail	Can identify main character	Can give detailed accounting of character and motive
	Skips over new words	New vocabulary impairs understanding	For new word, can give example but not definition	Can generate definition for new word or synonym
Motivated	Has limited interaction or response to reading	May be involved in or identify with portion of story	Responds on personal basis to selection	Tells others about what he/she has read
	Reads only when asked	Self-initiates reading	Has criteria for selecting reading materials	Analyzes personal choices and determines new selections to explore

Strategic	Is uncertain as to how all parts fit together but can identify parts of selections	Has structure for story reading	Understands criteria of expository piece	Differentiates fiction from non-fiction by structure of piece
Process (Before)	Simply begins reading; does not know purpose	Has purpose for reading but relies heavily on pictures	Demonstrates some knowledge of clues to use before reading (looks at graphics, predicts, asks questions)	Applies strategies before reading that help better understand what text will be about
(During)	Keeps reading if he/she docs not understand	Has only external strategies (will ask for help)	Uses some strategies during reading*	Applies appropriate strategies while reading; can self-correct**
(After)	Cannot verbalize about what he/she reads	Can identify which part he/she liked best	Can summarize with assistance/ direction	Summarizes accurately

*   Reading strategies: Summarizes and retells events, makes mental picture of what author says, predicts next event, alters predictions based on new information.

** Self-correction or "fix up" strategies: Looks back, looks ahead, rereads, slows down, asks for help.

Reading Rubric, Grade 3

Student Name: _____   School Year: _____

Campus: _____   Grade: _____

	Beginning	Developing	Capable	Expert
Fluent	Mispronounces common words	Sees word root and endings separately	Understands that prefixes, roots, and suffixes are "changeable parts"	Analyzes pronunciation using analogy to known words and word parts
	Decodes sentences haltingly	Decodes words accurately and automatically	Decodes words in context of paragraph	Reads with expression, fluency, and appropriate tone and pronunciation
Constructive	New vocabulary impairs understanding	Can generate example or synonym for new word	Can generate synonyms, definition, or antonyms for new word	Uses new and unusual words in writing or Speaking
	Predicts story based on pictures and other clues	Identifies parts of story in relation to his/her own experience	Connects personal experience to clues and text	Can compare and contrast previous personal experience to parts of story
Motivated	Reading is initiated by teacher	Self-initiates reading	Reads for pleasure	Reads for pleasure and information as needed
	Holds as much beginning information as possible and forgets rest	May describe what selection is about and provide some detail	Identifies main idea	Identifies main idea and supporting information
	Does not read for information	Reads for information if teacher-initiated	Uses appropriate text for needed information	Compares/ contrasts one piece of reading with/to another

Strategic	Has difficulty differentiating important from unimportant	Knows important parts exist; cannot always identify	Can identify important information	Can identify and store important information and discard unimportant
	Does not self-correct	Recognizes mistakes but has difficulty in self-correcting	Has strategies for self-correction**	Analyzes self-correction strategies as to best strategy**
Process (Before)	Prereading strategies involve number of pages and size of print	Identifies purpose for reading	Identifies purpose and applies strategies before reading that help better understand what text will be about	Determines strategies needed to understand selection
(During)	Calls words and skips words if they cannot be understood or pronounced	Some aspects of text are connected to prior knowledge/experience	Uses some strategies during reading*	Applies appropriate strategies while reading; can self-correct**
(After)	Summaries are retelling of as much as is remembered	Needs help with summary; can identify which part he/she liked best	Has strategy for categorizing and summarizing information	Organizes reading by sorting important from unimportant, then relating it to purpose and structure

* Reading strategies: Summarizes and retells events, makes mental picture of what author says, predicts next event, alters predictions based on new information.

** Self-correction or "fix up" strategies: Looks back, looks ahead, rereads, slows down, asks for help.

Reading Rubric, Grade 4

Student Name: _____   School Year: _____

Campus: _____   Grade: _____

	Beginning	Developing	Capable	Expert
Fluent	Mispronounces common words	Sees word root and endings separately	Understands that prefixes, roots, and suffixes are "changeable parts"	Analyzes pronunciation using analogies to known words and word parts
	Decodes sentences haltingly	Decodes words in context of paragraph	Decoding is non-issue	Reads with expression, fluency, and appropriate tone and pronunciation
Constructive	Can predict what character might do next	Can predict with some accuracy possible endings to story	Can predict more than one ending/solution	Can predict endings to story and explain advantages and disadvantages for author in using various endings
	New vocabulary impairs understanding	Can generate an example or synonym for new word	Can generate synonyms, definitions, or antonyms for new word	Uses new vocabulary in writing or speaking
Motivated	Has little understanding of reason for reading	Reads text because teacher said to	Establishes clear purpose for reading	Evaluates purpose for reading
	Has limited interaction with or response to reading	May mention character he/she has read about previously	Compares/ contrasts one piece of reading with/to another	Analyzes personal choices and determines new selections to explore

Strategic	Does not have enough information to ask questions	Has difficulty asking questions	Can ask questions about what was read	Asks questions that tie together this text and other reading
	Has difficulty differentiating important from unimportant	Can use structure to identify important information	Uses structure to assign, order, remember characters, and identify problem/goal	Uses structure to determine most important aspects of text to remember
	Has some difficulty differentiating the structure of fiction from non-fiction	Differentiates fiction from non-fiction by structure of piece	Can differentiate among structures used in fiction*	Can differentiate among non-fiction structures**
Process (Before)	Prereading strategies involve number of pages and size of print	Identifies purpose for reading	Applies strategies before reading that help better understand what text will be about	Determines strategies needed to better understand selection
(During)	Calls words and skips words if not understood	Some aspects of text are connected to prior knowledge/ experience	Uses some strategies during reading***	Applies appropriate strategies while reading; can self-correct****
(After)	Summaries are retelling of as much as is remembered	Can identify part he/she likes best but needs help with summary	Has strategy for categorizing information	Organizes reading by sorting important from unimportant and relating it to purpose and structure

* Fiction structures (examples): Flashbacks, chronological, episodic, story within story.

** Non-fiction structures (examples): Topical, cause and effect, sequential, comparison/contrast, persuasive.

*** Reading strategies: Summarizes and retells events, makes mental picture of what author says, predicts next event, alters predictions based on new information.

**** Self-correction or "fix up" strategies: Looks back, looks ahead, rereads, slows down, asks for help.

Reading Rubric, Grade 5

Student Name: _____   School Year: _____

Campus: _____   Grade: _____

	Beginning	Developing	Capable	Expert
Fluent	Rate of reading interferes with mean[ing]	Occasionally rate of reading interferes with meaning	Analyzes selection and uses most effective reading rate	Can articulate demands of reading task
Constructive	Has trouble understanding meaning of text	Can understand text but has difficulty formulating questions	Can explain why text is important and can summarize main points	Assigns meaning and relates information in larger context of knowledge
	Vocabulary slows reader	Can use text to make meaning of new vocabulary	Can ask questions about text	Applies vocabulary outside of text and uses it to refine understanding
Motivated	Does not read for information: concentrates on decoding	Holds as much beginning information as possible and forgets rest	Identifies main idea; determines fact and non-fact	Knows specific information he/she needs from text
	Can provide some details about selection	May describe what selection is about and provide some detail	Compares/ contrasts information with/to other events experiences	Develops questions unanswered by selection
	Reading is initiated by teacher	Reading is initiated by student	Shares reading with others	Actively seeks reading opportunities
Strategic	Differentiates fiction from non-fiction by structure of piece	Can differentiate among structures used in fiction*	Can differentiate among non-fiction structures**	Can articulate and analyze author's use of structure
Sorting	Can remember some of important pieces	Uses structure to assign order, remember characters, and identify problem/goal	Uses structures to determine most important aspects of text to remember	Discusses how structure assists reader in sorting important from unimportant

Asks questions	Does not have enough information to ask questions	Has difficulty asking questions	Can ask questions about what was read	Asks questions that tie this text to others
Self-correction strategies	Does not self-correct	Recognizes mistakes but has difficulty in self-correcting	Has strategies for self-correction****	Analyzes self-correction strategies as to best strategy****
Identifies purpose	Has little understanding of reason for reading	Reads text because teacher said to	Establishes clear purpose for reading	Evaluates purpose for reading
Process (Before)	Does not predict	Has some difficulty making predictions	Applies strategies before reading that help better understand what text will be about	Predicts and identifies how author or genre tends to end selections
(During)	Keeps reading if he/she does not understand	Uses some strategies during reading***	Applies appropriate strategies While reading; can self-correct****	Analyzes own reading and thinking while reading
(After)	Summaries are retelling of as much as is remembered	Has strategy for categorizing information	After reading, revises schema/conceptual organization	Develops more clarity in thinking as result of reading

* Fiction structures (examples): Flashbacks, chronological, episodic, story within story.

** Non-fiction structures (examples): Topical, cause and effect, sequential, comparison/contrast, persuasive.

*** Reading strategies: Summarizes and retells events, makes mental picture of what author says, predicts next event, alters predictions based on new information.

**** Self-correction or "fix up" strategies: Looks back, looks ahead, rereads, slows down, asks for help.

Math Rubric Examples

Missouri Assessment Program Scoring Guide

Mathematics

4 Points:	**The student's response fully addresses the performance event.** The response: • demonstrates knowledge of mathematical concepts and principles needed to complete the event. • communicates all process components that lead to appropriate and systematic solution. • may have only minor flaws with no effect on reasonableness of solution.
3 Points:	**The student's response substantially addresses performance event.** The response: • demonstrates knowledge of mathematical concepts and principles needed to complete event. • communicates most process components that lead to appropriate and systematic solution. • may have only minor flaws with minimal effect on reasonableness of solution.
2 Points:	**The student's response partially addresses the performance event.** The response: • demonstrates limited knowledge of mathematical concepts and principles needed to complete event. • communicates some process components that lead to appropriate and systematic solution. • may have flaws or extraneous information that indicates some lack of understanding or confusion.
1 Point:	**The student's response minimally addresses performance event.** The response: • demonstrates a limited knowledge of mathematical concepts and principles needed to complete the event. • communicates few or no process components that lead to appropriate and systematic solution. • may have flaws or extraneous information that indicates lack of understanding or confusion.
0 Points:	**The student's work consists of copying prompt information only, or the work indicates NO mathematical understanding of task.**

http://www.indep.k12.mo.us/pdc/MAPS/Math8/math_rubric.htm%20copy

207   Vermont Math Problem Solving Criteria

Source: **Vermont Department of Education**

Subjects:	*Mathematics*	*# of scales*	*4*
Grade(s)	*8*	*Scale length*	*4*

Scale 1: Understanding the Problem

4   Identified special factors that influenced the approach before starting the problem.
3   Understood the problem.
2   Understood enough to solve part of the problem or to get part of the solution.
1   Didn't understand enough to get started or make progress.

Scale II: How Student Solved Problem

4   Approach was efficient or sophisticated.
3   Approach would work for the problem.
2   Approach would only lead to solving part of the problem.
1   Approach didn't work.

Scale III: Decisions Along the Way

4   Clearly explained the reasons for the correct decisions made throughout the problem.
3   Didn't clearly explain the reasons for decisions, but work suggests correct reasoning used for only part of the problem.
2   Only partly correct reasoning, or correct reasoning used for only part of the problem.
1   No reasoning is evident from the work or reasoning is incorrect.

Scale IV: Outcomes of Activities

4   Solved the problem and made general rule about the solution or extended the solution to a more complicated situation.
3   Solved the problem and connected the solution to other math or described a use for what was learned in the "real world."
2   Only partly correct reasoning, or correct reasoning used for only part of the problem.
1   Solved the problem and stopped.

Chicago Public Schools Bureau of Student Assessment
http://intranet.cps.k12.il.us/Assessments/Ideas_and_Rubrics/Rubric_Bank/MathRubrics.pdf

211   Kentucky Holistic Scoring Rubric for Grade 12 Math

Source: **Kentucky Department of Education** *Open-Response Released Items and Scoring Rubrics: Grade 12* 1991-92

Subjects:	***Mathematics***	*# of Scales*	*1*
Grade(s)	***12***	*Scale length*	*5*

Holistic Scale

5   The student completes all important components of the task and communicates ideas clearly.

The student demonstrates in-depth understanding of the relevant concepts and/or processes.

Where appropriate, the student chooses more efficient and/or sophisticated processes.

Where appropriate, the student offers insightful interpretations or extensions (generalizations, applications, analogies).

4   The student completes most important components of the task and communicates clearly.

The student demonstrates understanding of major concepts even though he/she overlooks or misunderstands some less important ideas or details.

3   The student completes some important components of the task and communicates those clearly.

The student demonstrates that there are gaps in his/her conceptual understanding.

2   Student shows minimal understanding.

Student is unable to generate strategy, or answer may display only recall effect. Answer lacks clear communication.

Answer may be totally incorrect or irrelevant.

1   Blank/no response.

Chicago Public Schools Bureau of Student Assessment
http://intranet.cps.k12.il.us/Assessments/Ideas_and_Rubrics/Rubric_Bank/MathRubrics.pdf

218   Norwood Park Draft Math Problem-Solving Rubric (page 1 of 2)

Source: Faculty of Norwood Park Elementary School, Chicago, Illinois

Subjects:	*Mathematics*	***# of scales***	*5*
Grade(s)	*K-8*	***Scale length***	*4*

Scale I: Shows Evidence That Problem Was Understood

Distinguished   Shows rigorous understanding of the problem

Proficient   Shows substantial understanding of the problem

Apprentice   Shows limited understanding of the problem

Novice   Shows little or no understanding of the problem

Scale II: Uses Information Appropriately

Distinguished   Explains why certain information is essential to the solution

Proficient   Uses all appropriate information correctly

Apprentice   Uses some appropriate information correctly

Novice   Uses inappropriate information

Scale III: Applies Appropriate Procedures

Distinguished   Explains why procedures are appropriate for the problem

Proficient   Applies completely appropriate procedures

Apprentice   Applies some appropriate procedures

Novice   Applies inappropriate procedures

(cont'd)

Chicago Public Schools Bureau of Student Assessment
http://intranet.cps.k12.il.us/Assessments/Ideas_and_Rubrics/Rubric_Bank/MathRubrics.pdf

Source: Faculty of Norwood Park Elementary School, Chicago, Illinois

Scale IV: Uses Representations, e.g. Diagrams, Graphs, Pictures, Manipulatives, Equations

Distinguished Uses a representation that is unusual in its aesthetic value or mathematical precision

Proficient   Uses a representation that clearly depicts the problem

Apprentice   Uses a representation that gives some important information about the problem

Novice   Uses a representation that gives little or no significant information about the problem

Scale V: Shows Competent Use of Mathematics

Distinguished Makes a general rule about the solution that can be applied to another problem

Proficient   Shows complete competence in using mathematics

Apprentice   Shows some competence in using mathematics, skips some important steps, or omits some important information

Novice   Shows incompetent use of mathematics

Chicago Public Schools Bureau of Student Assessment
http://intranet.cps.k12.il.us/Assessments/Ideas_and_Rubrics/Rubric_Bank/MathRubrics.pdf

Source: Arizona Department of Education

Subjects:	*Mathematics*	***# of scales***	*3*
Grades(s)	*3-12*	***Scale length***	*5*

Holistic Scale

4   A 4 response represents an effective solution. It shows complete understanding of the problem, thoroughly addresses all points relevant to the solution, shows logical reasoning and valid conclusions, communicates effectively and clearly through writing and/or diagrams, and includes adequate and correct computations and/or setup. It may contain insignificant errors that do not interfere with the completeness or reasonableness of the student's response.

3   A 3 response contains minor flaws. Although it shows an understanding of the problem, communicates adequately through writing and/or diagrams, and generally reaches reasonable conclusions, it show minor flaws in reasoning and/or computation or neglects to address some aspect of the problem.

2   A 2 response shows gaps in understanding and/or execution. It shows one of some combination of the following flaws: an incomplete understanding of the problem, failure to address some aspects of the problem, faulty reasoning, weak conclusions, unclear communication in writing and/or diagrams, or a poor understanding of relevant mathematical procedures or concepts.

1   A 1 response shows some effort beyond restating the problem or copying given data. It shows some combination of the following flaws: little understanding of the problem, failure to address most aspects of the problem, major flaws in reasoning that lead to invalid conclusions, or a lack of understanding of relevant mathematical procedures or concepts.

0   A 0 response shows no mathematical understanding of the problem or the student has failed to respond to the item.

Chicago Public Schools Bureau of Student Assessment
http://intranet.cps.k12.il.us/Assessments/Ideas_and_Rubrics/Rubric_Bank/MathRubrics.pdf

Writing Rubrics

Grades 6-12

Developed by the Faculty of Goose Creek Consolidated Independent School District Baytown, Texas

SIXTH, SEVENTH, AND EIGHTH GRADES
PERSUASIVE – FIRST DRAFT

1-Below expectations
2-Minimum
3-Mastery
4-Excellent

Words found in prompt: State your position, convince

OBJECTIVES	1	2	3	4
1. Stays on topic	Addresses topic/ purpose in skeletal or general manner Drifts from topic/purpose (why to how-to) Information does not support position Responses are not persuasive	Addresses position and provides reasons Occasionally drifts from position/reasons	Remains on topic Response is consistent Persuades adequately	Presents convincing reasons in logical, unified manner Persuades convincingly
2. Organization and structure	Lacks connection between responses Rambles and/or is repetitive Major gaps and inconsistencies	Has introduction and a conclusion Organization apparent Some gaps, rambling, and inconsistencies	Generally well organized and clear enough to understand reasons presented Transition from one thought to another Has introduction, body, and conclusion Gives at least 3 reasons in body paragraphs	Clear sense of order and completeness Effective use of transitional elements Consistent organizational strategy evident Has introduction, body, and conclusion Gives at least 4 reasons in body paragraphs
3. Language control	Brief phrases Sentence fragments Illogical, confusing sentences Repeated errors in spelling usage and word choice	Awkward or simple sentences Many errors in spelling, capitalization, and punctuation do not affect understanding	Exhibits control of language Some grammatical errors interrupt flow of language Some variation in sentence structure Complete sentences	Consistent control of language Few, if any, grammatical errors Varied sentence construction, including compound and complex sentences

| 4. Support and elaboration | Insufficient elaboration to support position

Brief list of non-specific and unelaborated reasons

Minimal word choice | Some elaboration and/or extension of reasons

Number of specific reasons provided

Limited word choice | Elaboration may support 1 fully developed reason or a lengthy set of less-developed ideas

Effective word choice

Exhibits at least 2 types of elaboration | Specific and well-elaborated reasons that are clear and convincing

Rich, unusual, and/or vivid word choice

Exhibits 3 or more types of elaboration |

Scoring for editing and revisions for final draft.
Score **ONLY** the **FINAL COPY** of written compositions for mechanics, grammar, and conventions.
Before scoring, students should edit and revise their first draft for skills that have been taught.

OBJECTIVES	**1**	**2**	**3**	**4**
Mechanics, grammar, and conventions	Major errors in capitalization, punctuation, and spelling Incomplete sentences	Some errors in capitalization, punctuation, and spelling Some mistakes in subject-verb agreement Some sentence fragments	Minor revisions in spelling, capitalization Punctuation needed Usually uses correct subject-verb agreement	Capitalization, punctuation, and spelling acceptable for publication Subject-verb agreement correct
Fluency*	0-100	100-150	150-250	250+

* These figures represent an approximate number of words occurring in papers with these scores. However, the focus should be on elaborating ideas and not on counting words.

**SIXTH, SEVENTH, AND EIGHTH GRADES
COMPARE AND CONTRAST – FIRST DRAFT**

1-Below expectations
2-Minimum
3-Mastery
4-Excellent

CRITERIA	1	2	3	4
1. Stays on topic	Addresses topic/ purpose in skeletal or general manner Drifts from topic Writes for wrong purpose and mode	Addresses topic Provides adequate advantages/ disadvantages or similarities/ differences Writes for correct purpose/mode	May have slight inconsistency but is holistically consistent	Consistently stays on topic
2. Organization and structure	Lacks adequate number of similarities/ differences	Organization apparent Some gaps, rambling, and inconsistencies Gives 2 similarities and 2 differences Has introduction and may have conclusion	Generally well organized and clear enough to understand ideas presented Paragraphs indicate use of transition from one thought to another Evidence of introductory and concluding elements Gives at least 3 similarities and 3 differences	Presents at least 4 similarities/differ- ences or advantages/ disadvantages in logical manner Effective use of transitional elements Has introduction, body, and conclusion
3. Language control	No elaboration of ideas Attempts elaboration by explaining idea with only 1 sentence	Adequate number of ideas provided Minimal elaboration of ideas	Uses at least 2 methods of elaboration to support a single idea (i.e., simile, metaphor, example, analogy, anecdote, etc.) Slight repetition/ digression may occur	Elaborates in variety of ways (i.e., simile, metaphor, example, analogy, anecdote, etc.) Uses at least 3 methods of elaboration to support single idea

4. Language control	Numerous fragments or run-on sentences Illogical, confusing sentences Numerous errors in spelling, grammar, mechanics, writing conventions	Repeated errors in spelling, grammar, mechanics, writing conventions Awkward or simple sentences Limited word choice Some sentence fragments or run-on sentences	Exhibits control of language Some errors in spelling, grammar, mechanics, writing conventions Some variation in sentence structure Effective word choice	Consistent control of language Adheres to writing conventions Few, if any, errors in spelling, grammar, mechanics Varies sentence structure, including compound and complex sentences Rich, unusual, and vivid word choice
5. Special features*				

* To be added at teacher's discretion – first draft

SIXTH, SEVENTH, AND EIGHTH GRADES
DESCRIPTIVE – FIRST DRAFT

1-Below expectations
2-Minimum
3-Mastery
4-Excellent

CRITERIA	1	2	3	4
1. Stays on topic	Does not address topic Responses are not descriptive	Addresses topic and purpose in disorganized fashion Occasionally drifts	Stays on topic Presents description in order (sequential, topical)	Presents description in order (sequential, topical)
2. Organization and structure	Lacks connection Rambles Major gaps	Shows some sense of organization Some gaps, rambling, and inconsistencies	Has introduction, body, and conclusion Paragraphs indicate use of transition from one thought to another	Has introduction, body, and conclusion Shows strong sense of organizational strategy within paragraphs
3. Language control	Incomplete sentences Illogical, confusing sentences Repeated errors in spelling, grammar, and word choice	Awkward or simple sentences Many errors in spelling, grammar, and word choice Little use of adjectives and adverbs	Complete sentences Some variation in sentence structure Some errors in spelling, grammar, and word choice	Consistent control of language Few, if any, errors in spelling, grammar, word choice Varied sentence construction Excellent use of adjectives, adverbs
4. Support and elaboration	Insufficient elaboration to support description Minimal word choice Fails to address sensory details	Some elaboration Limited word choice Addresses details through 1 sense	Moderate elaboration Effective word choice Addresses details through 2 or 3 senses	Specific elaboration, which is highly descriptive and may include metaphors, similes, allusions, etc. Rich, unique word choice Vividly addresses sensory details using 4 or more senses

SIXTH, SEVENTH, AND EIGHTH GRADES
HOW-TO – FIRST DRAFT

1-Below expectations
2-Minimum
3-Mastery
4-Excellent

CRITERIA	1	2	3	4
1. Stays on topic	Directions are unclear/confusing Addresses topic in skeletal manner	Directions are stated Topic is somewhat related Occasionally drifts off subject	Directions are clearly stated and related throughout Remains focused	Directions are clearly stated, developed, and related throughout Remains focused
2. Organization and structure	No organization evident Much confusion and many inconsistencies Rambles and is repetitive Drifts off topic	Apparent organization and sequence Some inconsistencies Uneven use of transitions Has introduction and conclusion	Has introduction, body, and conclusion Most points logically sequenced Some transitions Occasional gaps in organization	Clear sense of order and completeness Sequences logically Appropriate/ sophisticated transitions Consistent and effective organization
3. Language control	Incomplete sentences Illogical, confusing sentences Major and/or repeated errors in spelling usage and word choice	Awkward, simple, and/or fragmented sentences Errors in spelling, capitalization, and punctuation, and subject-verb agreement	Exhibits control of language Some errors, such capitalization, punctuation, minor spelling errors, incorrect subject-verb agreement Some variation in sentence structure	Consistent control of language Few, if any, grammatical errors Varied sentence structure
4. Support and elaboration	Insufficient elaboration Few or no supporting points Inadequate word choice	Minimal elaboration Support is attempted Limited word choice	Process is presented partially through sequential steps Sufficient support Effective word choice	Process is presented effectively through sequential steps Elaboration for each step uses explanation, example, or detail

				Clear and convincing Rich, unusual, creative, and/or vivid choice of words
5. Reader appeal	Not interesting Confusing Awkward	Usual	Rather interesting Flows with minor gaps	Fluent Interesting, intriguing Creative/unusual Flows naturally

NINTH GRADE
CLASSIFICATORY – FIRST DRAFT

1-Below expectations
2-Minimum
3-Mastery
4-Excellent

CRITERIA	1	2	3	4
1. Stays on topic	Strays from topic Does not address or rarely addresses audience	Occasional deviations from topic Aware of but does not directly address audience	Stays on topic Most ideas/support are relevant Effectively addresses audience	No deviations from topic All support is extremely relevant Consistently addresses audience on appropriate level
2. Organization and structure	Presents only 1 side of issue Does not lead to logical conclusion	Has introduction, body, and conclusion Addresses both sides minimally Ideas do not progress logically toward conclusion Gives at least 3 similarities/differences or advantages/disadvantages	Has introduction, body, and conclusion Addresses both sides well Clear, logical progression of comparisons toward limited conclusion Gives at least 4 arguments on each side	Has introduction, body, and conclusion Clear sense of order in support of both sides of issues, ideas, topics Clear progression to logical conclusion Gives at least 5 arguments on each side
3. Language control	Brief phrases Sentence fragments Illogical, confusing sentences Repeated errors in spelling, usage, and word choice Minimal word choice	Awkward or simple but complete sentences Errors in spelling, capitalization, and punctuation have limited effect understanding Limited word choice	Few grammatical errors to interrupt flow Some variations in sentence structure Effective word choice	Uses appropriate transitional devices Consistent control of language Few grammatical errors Varied sentence structure Rich, vivid word choice

4. Support and elaboration	Insufficient elaboration to support both sides of topics, ideas, or issues	Some elaboration and/or extension of both sides of topics, issues, or ideas	Moderate elaboration of both sides of topics, issues, or ideas	Extensive elaboration of both sides of topics, issues, or ideas
	Brief lists of non-specific and unelaborated support of one or both sides	Gives elaboration for most similarities/ differences or advantages/ disadvantages	Elaborates each similarity/ difference and advantage/ disadvantage Elaboration includes citing specific examples from text, personal examples, quotes, etc.	Elaboration is rich, tied to each point, and promotes reader's understanding Elaboration includes citing specific examples from text, allowing notes, poetic devices, etc.
5. Special features*				

* To be added at teacher's discretion

NINTH AND TENTH GRADES
PERSUASIVE – FIRST DRAFT

1-Below expectations
2-Minimum
3-Mastery
4-Excellent

CRITERIA	1	2	3	4
1. Stays on topic	Strays from topic Does not address or rarely addresses audience	Deviates occasionally from topic Is aware of but does not directly address audience	Stays on topic Most ideas/ support are relevant Effectively addresses audience	Contains no deviations from topic Presents only relevant support Consistently addresses audience on appropriate level
2. Organization and structure	Lacks connection between ideas Has little or no paragraph structure Is repetitive	Shows apparent organization Contains some gaps, rambling, and inconsistencies Has introduction, body, and conclusion	Is generally well organized and clear enough to understand reasons presented Incorporates transition from one thought to another Has introduction, body, and conclusion	Contains clear sense of order and completeness Uses transitional elements effectively Incorporates organizational strategy that promotes and supports given argument Has introduction, body, and conclusion
3. Language control	Contains brief phrases and/or sentence fragments May contain illogical, confusing sentences Contains repeated errors in spelling, usage, and word choice Utilizes minimal word choice	Uses complete sentences that may be simple and/or awkward Contains errors in spelling, capitalization, and punctuation that have limited effect on understanding Utilizes limited word choice	Contains few grammatical errors that interrupt flow Exemplifies some variations in sentence structure Incorporates effective word choice	Uses appropriate transitional devices Shows consistent control of language Contains few grammatical errors Exemplifies varied sentence structure Incorporates rich, vivid word choice

| 4. Support and elaboration | Possesses insufficient elaboration to support position

Contains brief list of non-specific and unelaborated reasons | Exemplifies some elaboration and/or extension of reasons …

-OR-

Gives several specific reasons with minimal extension

Exhibits at least 3 types of elaboration | Contains moderately elaborated reasons to support stated choice …

-OR-

Gives effective elaboration to support 1 fully developed reason or lengthy set of less-developed ideas

Exhibits at least 5 types of elaboration | Presents specific and elaborated original reasons that are clear and convincing

Is clearly creative and is appealing to reader

Incorporates resource data that logically support the:

Contains elaboration that exemplifies advanced reasoning

Exhibits variety of appropriate types of elaboration |
|---|---|---|---|---|
| 5. Reason and logic | Does not contain logic/reasoning | Resembles list

Possesses little cohesiveness in argument | Uses closely aligned elaboration and organizational structure to support argument

Contains strong logic/reasoning pattern | Includes counter points of view and refutation

May use if …, then … pattern

Contains superior reasoning |

TENTH GRADE
TECHNICAL – FIRST DRAFT

1-Below Expectations
2-Minimum
3-Mastery
4-Excellent

CRITERIA	1	2	3	4
1. Stays on topic	Strays from topic Does not address or rarely addresses audience	Occasionally deviates from topic Is aware of but does not directly address audience Is clear about purpose	Stays on topic Most ideas/ support are relevant Effectively addresses audience as evidenced by word choice, formality, syntactical structure, etc.	May use purpose to persuade Does not deviate from topic Presents only relevant support Consistently addresses audience on appropriate level
2. Organization and structure	Is incomplete Is ineffective, rambling Has inappropriate format for purpose	Presents information but does not communicate effectively Uses appropriate format	Effectively communicates ideas Uses appropriate format Contains effective format	Presents information expediently Uses appropriate format Closely ties all parts of report/format to purpose
3. Language control	Uses brief phrases or sentence fragments May use illogical, confusing sentences Makes repeated errors in spelling, usage, and word choice Utilizes limited word choice	Uses complete sentences that may be simple and/or awkward Makes errors in spelling, capitalization, and punctuation that do not affect understanding Utilizes limited word choice	Contains few grammatical error that interrupt flow Exemplifies some variations in sentence structure Incorporates effective word choice	Uses appropriate transitional devices Shows consistent control of language Contains few grammatical errors Exemplifies varied sentence structure Incorporates rich, vivid word choice

4. Support and elaboration	Is ineffective Does not convey intended message	Conveys intended message but is incomplete Is somewhat effective Addresses key points, but appropriate support is missing or uneven	Is complete and effective but wordy Uses graphics, charts, data, etc., to elaborate key points Uses appropriate examples, reasons, data, and graphics for audience	Is complete and succinct Incorporates elaboration that exemplifies advanced reasoning Presents support and elaboration for ease of reader

ELEVENTH AND TWELFTH GRADES
LITERARY ANALYSIS, CHARACTER, SETTING, THEME – ANY OF 8 OR COMBINATION; SENIORS MUST USE CONFLICT

	1	2	3	4
1. Stays on topic	Rambles from idea to idea	Occasionally drifts Some consistency on topic	Remains on topic Response is consistent	Logical, unified, and coherent manner Remains on topic with logic
2. Organization and structure	Little or no order No transitions No topic sentences	Organization apparent with gaps and flaws Some transitions Some use of topic sentences Has introduction, body, and conclusion	Organization apparent, with some flaws Uses transitions Topic sentences Has developed introduction, body, and conclusion but may be uneven	Clear and effective transitions Topic sentences enhance argument Has well and evenly developed introduction, body, and conclusion, all of which catch reader's attention
3. Language control	Simple sentences and fragments Major spelling and mechanical problems Minimal word choice	Simple sentences used Errors in mechanics and spelling impede understanding Consistent "being" verbs	Some sentence variation Some errors in mechanics Some "being" verbs	Varied and effective sentence usage Few, if any, grammatical errors Few "being" verbs Rich and varied word choice
4. Support and elaboration	No support No elaboration Minimal word choice Unelaborated points Must satisfy need for character, setting, or theme in elaboration (12th grade must add conflict)	Limited word choice Some commentary, usually brief Elaboration may be 1 fully developed reason May use proof	All reasons elaborated but not fully Two types of elaboration Some proof from text Must satisfy need for character, setting, or theme in elaboration (12th grade must add conflict)	Consistent use of proofs from text Every reason elucidated fully, with varied types of elaboration Satisfies need for character, setting, or theme in elaboration (12th grade must add conflict)

	No voice or purpose	Must satisfy need for character, setting, or theme in elaboration (12th grade must add conflict) Attempted voice and purpose	Author's voice and/or purpose is included in elaboration	Author's voice or purpose is argued/refuted persuasively
5. Reason and logic	Logic/reasoning not present	Key points resemble list Little cohesiveness in argument	Elaboration and organizational structure are used to support argument, and all are closely aligned Logic/reasoning pattern is strong	Counter points of view are included and refuted May use if …, then… pattern Reasoning is superior

ELEVENTH AND TWELFTH GRADES
TECHNICAL ANALYSIS/DESCRIPTIVE PROBLEM-SOLVING (REAL-LIFE SITUATION)

CRITERIA	1	2	3	4
1. Stays on topic	Rambles from idea to idea Does not address audience or purpose	Occasionally drifts Some consistency on topic Is clear about audience and purpose	Remains on topic Response is consistent Addresses audience effectively as evidenced by word choice, formality, syntactical structure, etc.	Logical, unified, and coherent manner Remains on topic with logic Consistently addresses audience on appropriate level
2. Organization and structure	Little or no order No transitions No topic sentences Organizational pattern for analysis and problem-solving not present	Organization includes overview of situation Some analysis or problem-solving present but no clear pattern Some transitions Some use of topic sentences	Organization includes overview, as well as key points of analysis/problem-solving Uses transitions Topic sentences are tied to organizational pattern May include recommendations in conclusion	Clarity of overview and key points Patterns of analysis/problem-solving are clear and have impact Clear and effective transitions Topic sentences enhance delivery of key points
3. Language control	Simple sentences and fragments Major spelling and mechanical problems Minimal word choice	Simple sentences used Errors in mechanics and spelling impede understanding Consistent "being" verbs	Some sentence variation Some errors in mechanics Some "being" verbs	Varied and effective sentence usage Few, if any, grammatical errors Few "being" verbs Rich and varied word choice

4. Support and elaboration	No support No elaboration Analysis/problem-solving not present, but may be restatement of information from text or sources Unelaborated points	Some commentary, usually brief Elaboration may be 1 fully developed reason May use proofs	All points elaborated but not fully Two types of elaboration Some proofs from text Pattern of support is clear but unevenly developed	Consistent use of proofs from text Every point elucidated fully, with varied types of elaboration Support central to argument Pattern of support is clear and sound
5. Reason and logic	Very little logic or reasoning present	Analysis is limited Reasoning based on personal perspective rather than text/data Points/support overgeneralized or off mark	Reasoning/logic is accurate Overall reasoning pattern fits argument Data/text used are directly linked to pattern of analysis/problem-solving	Reasoning/logic is complete and accurate May extrapolate on analysis, e.g., if…, then… Reasoning/logic is interwoven with organizational structure and support

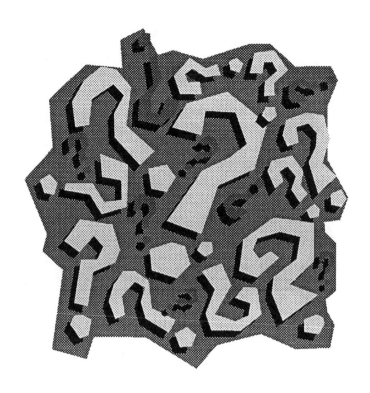

Ten-Question Tests

Teachers of the same subject and grade at elementary level or same course at secondary level meet together and write 10 questions that assess the standards taught during that grading period; questions are written in the format of the state assessment. Teachers agree to include these on the six or nine week test (or unit test if end-of-grading-period tests are not given). Teachers can include other questions on the test, if they wish. After assessing the students, teachers meet together to review student performance on the common items. The question is, "Are students making progress toward the standards?"

GRADE 3 - SECOND SIX WEEKS

1. Bill has $37. He earned $10 more mowing grass. Then he spent $14. Which shows how to find the amount of money Bill had left?

    ☞ 37 + 10 + 14 =
    ☞ 37 + 10 - 14 =
    ☞ 37 - 10 - 14 =
    ☞ 37 - 10 + 14 =

2. Sam has 703 baseball cards. His uncle gave him 317 cards. How many baseball cards does Sam have in all?

    ☞ 1,010
    ☞ 1,100
    ☞ 1,020
    ☞ 1,200

3. There are 78 boys in third grade. There are 83 girls. Which expression shows how many more girls than boys are in third grade.

    ☞ 78 - 83 =
    ☞ 78 + 83 =
    ☞ 83 - 78 =
    ☞ 83 + 78 =

4. There are 273 students in second grade, 320 in third grade, and 297 in fourth grade. How many students were in the three grades combined?

         ☞ 780 students
         ☞ 880 students
         ☞ 890 students
         ☞ 990 students

5. The graph represents the number of pieces of fruit in the basket.

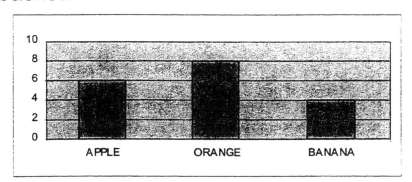

Which chart matches the graph.

○
FRUIT	apple	orange	banana
NUMBER	5	7	3

○
FRUIT	apple	orange	banana
NUMBER	6	8	4

○
FRUIT	apple	orange	banana
NUMBER	1	3	2

Look at the graph. The graph shows the number of books sold last week at Tom's Bookstore.

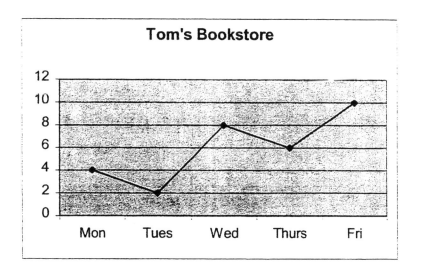

6. On which day did Tom sell the most number of books?

☞ Mon
☞ Wed
☞ Fri

7. On which day did Tom sell the least number of books?

☞ Mon
☞ Tues
☞ Wed

8. Kelly spent $38 on a new dress. She spent $19 on a pair of shoes. Which is the best estimate to show how much Kelly spent in all?

☞ $40
☞ $50
☞ $60
☞ $70

9. Mrs. Felder is going to buy popsicles for her class on Friday. She has 24 students. There are 10 popsicles in each box. How many boxes does Mrs. Felder need to buy so that each student has one?

☞ 2 boxes
☞ 3 boxes
☞ 4 boxes
☞ 5 boxes

10. Mad Minute exercise. Solve 30 problems in one minute.

Process 4: Select Systemic Interventions

What are systemic interventions?

A. Content

Select programs for effectiveness, high payoff for time spent, meeting more than one requirement at a time.

B. Time

1. Adjusting/adapting master schedule

2. Changing time allocations for subject

3. Providing more time for student

4. Establishing linkages between programs

C. Relationships

Increasing one-on-one time

D. Abstractions

1. Registers of language

2. Mental models

REGISTERS OF LANGUAGE

REGISTER	EXPLANATION
FROZEN	Language that is always the same. For example: Lord's Prayer, wedding vows, etc.
FORMAL	The standard sentence syntax and word choice of work and school. Has complete sentences and specific word choice.
CONSULTATIVE	Formal register when used in conversation. Discourse pattern not quite as direct as formal register.
CASUAL	Language between friends and is characterized by 400- to 800-word vocabulary. Word choice general and not specific. Conversation dependent upon non-verbal assists. Sentence syntax often incomplete.
INTIMATE	Language between lovers or twins. Language of sexual harassment.

Process 5: Embedding Monitoring Strategies

Plan your interventions/monitoring for the school year

July	August	September
October	November	December
January	February	March
April	May	June

Embed the dates into your campus calendar

MONTH

Monday	Tuesday	Wednesday	Thursday	Friday

APPENDICES

Utilizing the Training

Implementation

1. Which workshop activities do I still need to complete?

2. What is my plan to share this training with other staff members?

3. What steps must I take to implement the training?

4. What will be my timeline for implementing training components?

5. How will I measure results?

6. What is my timeline for reviewing the included resources?

7. What additional information do I need?

QUESTIONS TO ASK TO IMPROVE TEST PERFORMANCE

1. Do the questions on the test reflect what is taught in the classroom? How frequently are students exposed to this information/skill?

2. What is the breakdown in the data by student number by quartile? In other words, how many students fell in the bottom one-fourth of scores, etc.? Look at the specific students in the bottom quartile and the top quartile. Are those the students you would expect in those quartiles? If not, why not? If so, that would need to be done to move them into the next quartile?

3. Sometimes students who do poorly have the subject-area skills, but not test-taking skills. Do a mock test. Is it an issue of pacing, improper placement of answers, not finishing, negative self-talk, format, or not understanding the questions?

4. What objectives are not being mastered? How many more questions would each student need to answer correctly to master? (Getting none out of four correct is different from two out of four.) Is there a pattern at the grade level? At the classroom level?

5. Is the student missing more questions toward the end of the test? (Fatigue, fading concentration, harder problems?) Does the individual student have a pattern?

6. What is the ethnic breakdown of the data? How are the whites, blacks, and Hispanics doing in comparison with each other? If there is a major discrepancy, what might be reasons contributing to it? How can resources be reallocated to address the discrepancy?

7. For those students doing poorly, what is the amount of parental involvement? What training can be provided to parents?

8. What is the attendance pattern for the student? Poor attendance and low achievement often go together. What can you do to encourage attendance?

9. How familiar is the student with the test format? Format familiarity can affect up to 50% of a student's score on a test.

10. At the secondary level, what motivates the student to master the test?

MEASURING GROWTH

1. If you have an aptitude score for a student (it can be obtained easily by the group administering the Developing Cognitive Abilities Test, what is the relationship between the aptitude stanine and the achievement stanine? Is the student underachieving?

2. Is the student reaching his/her potential? If a student has an aptitude of 130, one would expect 1.3 years of growth in a given year. Likewise, if it were a mainstreamed student with an aptitude of 70, one would expect 0.7 years of growth. This is based on the notion that a reasonable expectation for a 100 aptitude score would be one year's growth.

3. Disaggregate data are based on a sample of students who have been in the district program for three years. Data should indicate that they are maintaining their level of performance within 5 percentage points of their original score or same percentage of mastery over time. If the aggregate data indicate that the scores are dropping each year, curriculum and programs need to be examined.

4. What assessments can be put into place at the end of each semester or year to monitor progress? These might include portfolios, rubrics, contests, performance assessments, DCAT, etc.

5. For what percentage of students is it reasonable to expect mastery of objectives? Calculate based on individual students currently enrolled, as well as where you would like to set goals.

QUESTIONS TO ASK FOR READING IMPROVEMENT

1. How many of the questions are text-dependent? In other words, are the answers in the text? How many of these text-dependent questions did the student miss? If several, the issue may be in not carefully reading the text.

2. How many of the questions are text-independent? In other words, the answers come in part from the information a student has in his/her head? If the student misses these types of questions, the student may not have sufficient concept development, problem-solving strategies, or skills in making generalizations or connections.

3. In non-fiction, can the student categorize the information? If not, the ability to comprehend will be quite limited.

4. Can the student formulate questions regarding the reading? If not, the ability to comprehend is probably limited.

5. Is the issue one of vocabulary? Often context is not all that helpful in determining vocabulary. What instruction occurs in vocabulary?

6. In which areas did the majority of students do poorly? Is this representative of the weaknesses of the curriculum?

7. How much time are students given to read daily? Studies indicate that if a student reads only two stories a week, he/she is not reading enough to understand story structure, which is a key component in comprehension. In other words, if students do not understand how stories fit together, their ability to comprehend will be limited. One-third of the time devoted to reading instruction should be spent with students reading. At the secondary level, a great deal of independent reading should be occurring (four to six novels/texts assigned annually).

8. What is the quality of texts that students are reading? Are the selections chopped, bland, limited in meaning, missing key cause-effect connections, not connected to experiences the students might have? What opportunities do students have to write and tell their own stories, draw/illustrate stories, summarize stories, etc.?

9. How much time is spent on skill sheets? According to the Center for the Study of Reading, University of Illinois, no more than one-fourth of all time allotted to reading should be spent on skill sheets.

10. What kind of interventions are made in the first and second grade for those students who are having difficulty reading? (Interventions in reading make the most difference in grades 1 and 2.) How can the schedule be rearranged so that additional time is available? What personnel resources can be utilized differently?

11. Can the child actually read (i.e., decode the words)?

QUESTIONS TO ASK TO IMPROVE WRITING PERFORMANCE

1. How frequently are students writing? Students should write daily, and it can include journal writing, stories, essays, drawings (especially young children), etc. This should begin in kindergarten.

2. In analyzing the writing, which of the following are issues? Fluency, organization, focus, sentence variety, reasoning, sentence structure, grammar, content, elaboration, etc.

3. Is writing regarded as important? In what ways is writing rewarded and honored? Do students have an opportunity to read to other students what they write?

4. How is writing progress measured? Are portfolios kept? Is the writing periodically checked against rubrics? What systematic methods are used to look at writing over time?

5. How much time allocated for writing is spent teaching grammar? Studies indicate a negative correlation between writing and grammar instruction. Students need to know enough grammar to edit their writing but not at the expense of their writing time.

QUESTIONS TO ASK TO IMPROVE MATH PERFORMANCE

1. What is the amount of time spent on review at each grade level? Do students have the opportunity to learn all facets of math? How much of the time is devoted to computational skills rather than conceptual and problem-solving development?

2. How much homework is given and in what amounts? (Five problems work as well as 20.)

3. Is problem-solving done daily?

4. In what areas is the student having the most difficulty? Does the curriculum address those areas?

5. Are manipulatives used? How is the student taught to transfer the concepts learned with manipulatives to paper-pencil activities?

6. Is the student encouraged to draw out solutions to the problem and/or use different processes?

7. On the test, do the questions involve multiple operations and multiple steps? Are those kinds of questions asked as part of class work?

8. Are the errors related to accuracy, misunderstanding of the problem, incorrect operations, missed or incorrect steps/processes, or not finishing the test? (Some computational tests require that students do three problems a minute in sixth grade, for example.) What are the test's speed requirements?

9. Do students write as part of mathematics?

10. Are students allowed to use calculators?

11. At the secondary level, have the course sequences helped or hurt students acquire the information and skills necessary for the test?

SUGGESTED STAFF DEVELOPMENT

What makes a difference in achievement?

1. **Cooperative Learning**: Joyce, Showers and Rolheiser-Bennett indicate that when properly implemented, cooperative learning can provide one standard deviation of growth in one year (i.e. 15 percentage points on a norm-referenced test). Generally, growth of 5% in one year is considered exceptional.

2. **TESA** (Teacher Expectations and Student Achievement): This is a peer-coaching model that in the studies promoted a four-grade-level growth in reading in one year. It looks at 15 student-teacher interactions that teachers use with high-achieving students. When it's used with all students, achievement increases, and student absences decrease.

3. **Tactics for Thinking**: This training is based on cognitive research and involves more than 20 skills that studies indicate make a difference in learning and achievement. These include learning-to-learn skills (taking responsibility, attitude, memory, etc.) and skills related to information processing and internal organization (concept attainment, concept development, reasoning, etc.). In particular, using graphic organizers as a part of instruction allowed most students to achieve as well as those students normally receiving 90%.

4. **Project Read**: Provides a multi-sensory approach to decoding and beginning reading.

5. **Reciprocal Teaching**: Ann Marie Palinscar has found that teaching students to ask questions could significantly raise comprehension.

6. **Process Writing and/or Written Expression**: A process for teaching writing that takes into account the developmental stages of writing and the processes that writers use.

7. **Peer Coaching**: Promotes the most teacher change and growth. This is staff development in which teachers observe each other teaching – and give feedback against given criteria. These data are not shared with the principal, only with the teacher observed.

8. **Math Manipulatives**: Make a difference in conceptual development and promote higher achievement when appropriate transfer techniques also are taught as part of the process.

9. **Reading Recovery**: A very effective and expensive program. Ninety percent of all students who have received the intervention in first grade never need reading assistance again.

10. **Specific Subject Area Techniques**: Shulman and Berliner have found that the specific representation used to teach a subject or skill is very important in achievement.

11. **Inquiry Approach**: Joyce, Showers, and Rolheiser-Bennett report increased achievement using the inquiry approach.

ACTIVITIES TO DO WITH STUDENTS

1. Flexible sub-grouping of students: Slavin indicates that when students are pre-tested and sub-grouped for a particular skill, higher achievement results. This achievement does not occur if the students are locked into a group.

2. Tracking decreases achievement for the lower half of the class.

3. Amount of time on task and feedback/collectives have a significant correlation with achievement. Benjamin Bloom has found those two to be significant in achievement. In the effective school, 80% of the time is on task. In an average school, it is 70% or less. Have teachers monitor the amount of time taken away from instruction by waiting in line, taking attendance, etc. How specific is the feedback? What correctives are provided?

4. The long-term goals a teacher sets for students are more important in achievement than the daily objectives. For example, by the end of the year, I expect my students to ...

5. Vocabulary development: Vocabulary is directly tied to all IQ testing and high-test scores. Vocabulary also assists with the categories set up in the brain to store information (schemata). A systematic vocabulary program can raise aptitude scores and does raise reading scores.

6. Having students read and write: The most direct correlation for high achievement in reading and writing is the actual amount of time students spend reading and writing. Using the inquiry approach in writing provides one-half standard deviation in growth in a year.

Have students become familiar with the test format. Do sample questions daily. Also provide opportunities for students to do a "dry run" (i.e., the complete format as it would be presented during a test.) Talk about how they approached questions, the self-talk they used, how they dealt with fatigue, what they did when they didn't know an answer, how they paced themselves, etc.

Campuswide Interventions That Improve Student Achievement

By Ruby Payne, Ph.D.
Educational Consultant

"With simpler models of staff development that are operational and involve 100 percent of the staff, the roller coaster ride that students take through school can be significantly lessened."

Conversation between a principal new to the building and a supervisor:

Supervisor: "That campus cannot be low-performing again. I do not have any extra money to give you. With the Title 1 money you have at your campus, your school will need to find a way to raise your achievement significantly."

Principal (to herself as she walks to the car): "And just how would that happen? I have 1,100 students, 80 percent low income, 12 new teachers, a mobility rate of 40 percent. I know it can be done, but in a year?"

Many of our models for staff development and curriculum development do not address realities pressuring schools today. Some of these realities are:

• The critical mass needed to impact student achievement. Example: Ninety percent of teachers are doing a particular intervention or strategy versus 10 percent doing it.

• The growing knowledge base required of teachers and administrators. Example: Educators are to know about sexual harassment, inclusion, cooperative learning, reading strategies, ADHD, modifications, gifted/talented strategies, legal guidelines, ESL strategies, etc.

• The time frames in which student achievement is to occur and be measured. Example: State and norm-referenced tests are designed for annual measures of learning.

• The accountability criteria that schools must meet. Example: In Texas, AEIS data and TAAS data are used to determine accreditation status.

• The lack of money and time for extensive training for teachers. Example: Most districts and campuses have five days or less of staff development, which limits the length and/or depth of the training.

• The increased numbers of students who come from poverty and/or who lack support systems at home. Example: Educated parents, when the school system does not address their children's needs, tend to provide assistance, pay for a tutor, or request a teacher. In poverty, the student only gets interventions through school.

• The increased number of new

teachers spurred by the increase in the school-age population. Example: The school-age population in America will increase by 25 percent in the next decade.

Processes and models are available to address these needs. But to do so, an additional model for staff development and curriculum development must be used. This model basically trades in-depth learning for critical mass by using a simpler approach. Fullan talks about the importance of critical mass as well as the main criteria teachers use to determine how "user-friendly" the curriculum and training are, i.e., how operational they are. (Fullan, 1991; Fullan, 1996)

In these models, which I have used for several years, the amount of time spent in training is decreased, the model is less complex and totally operational, and 100 percent of the staff is trained. *We still need reflective staff development*; we just need an additional model to help address some of the issues above.

Figure A outlines some of the basic differences.

What does this information mean in practice? With simpler models that are operational and involve 100 percent of the staff, the roller coaster ride that students take through school can be significantly lessened. One of the reasons that middle-class students do better in school is that their parents intervene to lessen the impact of the roller coaster. (These parents do so by paying for tutoring, requesting teachers and providing assistance and instruction at home.)

As you can see in Figure B, the X represents Johnny and his journey through five years of school. In first grade, he had a wonderful teacher who willingly went to every kind of training available. Johnny had a great year and made the expected progress.

In second grade, his teacher was having many health problems

Figure A

	Reflective Staff Development	Operational Staff Development
Definition	A process by which a person examines in-depth his learning on a given subject	A method for immediate implementation across the system to address accountability and student achievement
Purpose	To build in-depth learning and change	To impact the system quickly; to build in connections/linkages across the system
Effects of critical mass	Depends on amount of resources and level of attrition; takes at least four to five years	Affects critical mass almost immediately; can have 80 to 90 percent implementation the first year
Time required	Four to five days per person for initial training	Two hours to one day of training per person
Breadth	Limited	Systemic
Cost analysis	High per-person cost	Low per-person cost
District role	May be contacted or may use district expertise to deliver and provide follow-up	Identify with campuses system needs to be addressed. Works with campuses to reach critical mass. Assists with the operational development of innovation
Follow-up	Provided in small groups or by expert trainer	Provided through accountability measures and the fine tuning from discussions to make innovation more user-friendly
Role of principal	Is liason with training. May provide resources and follow-up opportunities	Assists with the delivery of training. Provides the insistence, support and accountability for innovation

Figure B

Johnny's progress	Grade 1	Grade 2	Grade 3	Grade 4	Grade 5
Grade 1	X				
Grade 2	X				
Grade 3			X		
Grade 4		X			
Grade 5					

and missed quite a few days of school. In addition, Johnny's parents divorced so he was shuttled between homes. In the second grade, Johnny actually regressed.

In the third grade, he had a beginning teacher. She loved the students but did not have the experience or the guidelines to provide the instruction that the other third-grade teacher did. Most of the educated parents had asked for the other teacher because of her excellent reputation. Johnny made progress.

In the fourth grade, Johnny had a teacher who did not participate in staff development. As far as she was concerned, it was a waste of time. Her students tended to do poorly on the state test, but her husband was on the school board. Once again, given her reputation, the educated parents had requested that their children be placed in the other fourth-grade classroom.

In the fifth grade, it was determined that Johnny was now two-and-a-half grade levels behind and should possibly be tested for special education.

How can we address this problem? With systemic interventions that can impact achievement through simple yet effective tools and processes.

Benjamin Bloom (1976) did extensive research to determine what makes a difference in learning. He identified four factors: 1) the amount of time to learn; 2) the intervention(s) of the teacher; 3) how clear the focus of the instruction is; and 4) what the student came in knowing. As is readily apparent, the control the individual teacher has over these variables is significantly impacted by what is happening at the campus. When these interventions are addressed at a campus level in a systematic way, more learning occurs.

Systemic interventions that can impact achievement are:

1. *Reasonable expectations.* This is a simpler model of curriculum mapping that addresses the focus of instruction and the amount of time.

2. *Growth assessments.* These are methods for identifying and assessing the growth a student makes on a regular basis.

3. *Benchmarks.* This is a simpler model of three to four indicators by grading period to show whether a student needs an immediate intervention. *It is absolutely crucial for first-grade reading.* Honig (1995) states that a first-grader who is not in the primer by April of the first-grade year generally does not progress beyond the third-grade reading level.

4. *Interventions for the student.* When students are identified through the growth assessments and benchmarks as making inadequate growth, immediate interventions are provided for the student, one of which is allowing more time during the school day.

What follows is a description and example for each of the above. *It is important to note that all of these are working documents of one or two pages so that they can constantly be reassessed.* It is analogous to having a road map: all of the details are not present. However, the lay of the land, the choices of the route and the final destination are clear.

Reasonable expectations

Reasonable expectations identify what is taught and the amount of time devoted to it. This allows a campus to "data mine," i.e., determine the payoff between what actually gets taught, the

Figure C

> ## Simple Yet Effective Tools and Processes
>
> One of the first pieces of information that a principal and campus need to know is *what is actually being taught.* Here's a simple process to help find this out:
>
> 1. If you are on a six-weeks grading period, divide a paper into six equal pieces. If you are on a nine-weeks grading period, divide a paper into four equal pieces. Have each teacher for each subject area write the units or skills that they teach in each grading period. In other words, what do they usually manage to teach to that grade level in that subject area in that amount of time?
>
> 2. Have each grade level meet and discuss one subject area at a time. Do all the teachers at a grade level basically have the same expectations for that grade level in terms of content and skills? Have they come to a consensus about the expectation for that grade level?
>
> 3. Have the faculty as a group compare the grade levels one through five or six through eight or nine through 12. If Johnny was with the school for five years, what would he have the opportunity to learn? What would he not have had the opportunity to learn? Where are the holes in the opportunities to learn?
>
> 4. The faculty then uses this information to identify the strengths and weaknesses in the current educational program. Are some things repeated without benefit to achievement? Are some things not ever taught or so lightly brushed to not be of benefit? What is included that could be traded out for something that has a higher payoff in achievement?
>
> 5. When the discussion is over, the one-page sheets are revised and given to the appropriate teachers.
>
> 6. Twice a year, the principal meets with grade-level teams, and using these sheets, discusses the progress of the learning, adjustments that need to be made, etc. These become working documents, and because of their simplicity, they can be easily revised.

amount of time given to it and the corresponding test results. For example, if two hours a day are spent on reading but only 15 minutes is devoted to students actually reading, the payoff will be less than if 45 minutes of that time is devoted to students actually reading.

Figure C is the process used. For each subject area, it requires about 30 to 60 minutes of individual time, one to two hours of grade-level time and three hours of total faculty time.

Figure D is an example from Runyan Elementary in Conroe, Texas. The principal is Nancy Harris.

Growth assessments

There are any number of growth assessments available. What makes something a growth assessment is that it identifies movement against a constant set of criteria. What makes a growth assessment different from a test is that the criteria do not change in a growth assessment. Rubrics are one way to measure and identify growth.

Figure E is an example of a reading rubric to measure student growth. It was developed by Sandra Duree, Karen Coffey and myself in conjunction with the teachers of Goose Creek ISD. *Becoming a Nation of Readers* identified characteristics of skilled readers, so those characteristics were used to measure growth as a constant over five years. We identified what growth would look like over five years if a student were progressing as a skilled reader.

To develop a growth assessment, a very simple process can be used. Have the teachers in your building (who consistently get the highest achievement, understand the district curriculum and TAAS specs) develop the growth assessment. Keep in mind these guidelines: 1) the purpose is to identify the desired level of achievement; 2) the growth assessment needs to be simple and easily understood;

Figure D

Second Grade Language Arts Curriculum
(70 percent fiction, 30 percent nonfiction)

First six weeks
Reading—60 minutes
DEAR—10 minutes
Teacher reading to students
Reading workshop—50 minutes

Spelling—60 words total
10 words per week

Writing—45 minutes
Personal narrative two to three
    sentences same subject
DOL—15 minutes
Writing workshop—30 minutes

*Vocabulary (integrated)—5 words
per week*

Skills—20 minutes
Choosing a just right book
Characters
Predicting
Distinguishing between fiction
    and nonfiction

Second six weeks
Reading—60 minutes
DEAR—10 minutes
Teacher reading to students
Reading workshop—50 minutes

Spelling—60 words total
10 words per week

Writing—45 minutes
Six to seven lines on same
    subject for how-to
DOL—15 minutes
Writing workshop—30 minutes

*Vocabulary (integrated)—5 words
per week*

Skills—20 minutes
Setting
Beginning, Middle, End of Story
Parts of speech: noun, verb
Sequential order
Comprehension
Compound words
Contractions

Third six weeks
Spelling—60 words total
10 words per week

Writing—45 minutes
Five to seven steps in paragraph,
    sequential for how-to
DOL—15 minutes
Writing workshop—30 minutes

*Vocabulary (integrated)—5 words
per week*

Skills—20 minutes
Main idea
Prefix, suffix
Context clues
Synonyms, antonyms, homo-
    phones, homony
Comprehension
Compound words
Contractions

Fourth six weeks
Reading—60 minutes
DEAR—15 minutes
Teacher reading to students
Reading workshop—45 minutes

*Spelling—15 minutes—60 words
total*
10 words per week
ABC order to second letter

Writing—45 minutes
How-to five to seven steps in
    paragraph form
DOL—15 minutes TAAS form
Writing workshop—30 minutes

*Vocabulary (integrated)—5 words
per week*

Skills—20 minutes
Quotes
Draw conclusions
Make inferences
Adjectives/adverbs
Comprehension
Possessives
Compound words
Contractions

Fifth six weeks
Reading—60 minutes
DEAR—15 minutes
Teacher reading to students
Reading workshop—45 minutes

*Spelling—15 minutes—60 words
total*
10 words per week
ABC order to third letter

Writing—45 minutes
Descriptive writing—7 sentences
Compare/contrast
DOL—15 minutes TAAS form
Writing workshop—30 minutes

*Vocabulary (integrated)—5 words
per week*

Skills—20 minutes
Main idea distinguished from
    details
Fact/opinion
Cause/effect
Comprehension
Possessives
Compound words
Contractions

Sixth six weeks
Reading—60 minutes
DEAR—15 minutes
Teacher reading to students
Reading workshop—45 minutes

*Spelling—15 minutes—60 words
total*
10 words per week
ABC order to third letter

Writing—45 minutes
Summary
Compare/contrast
DOL—15 minutes TAAS form
Writing workshop—30 minutes

*Vocabulary (integrated)—5 words
per week*

Skills—20 minutes
Recognize propoganda and point
    of view
Comprehension
Possessives
Compound words
Contractions

and 3) student movement or growth toward the desired level of achievement needs to be clear.

These are the steps to creating a growth assessment:

1. Identify three to five criteria.

2. Set up a grid with numerical values. (One through four is usually enough.)

3. Identify what would be an excellent piece of work or demonstration. That becomes number four.

4. Work backwards: Next identify what would be a three and so on.

When the growth assessment is developed, it needs to go back to the faculty for feedback and refinement. When there is substantial agreement and 80 percent buy-in, the faculty needs to move forward with it.

Benchmarks

Figure F is one example. As you can see from the ex-

Figure E

Reading Rubric Grade 1

Student name: _____ School Year: _____

Campus: _____ Grade: _____

	Beginning	Developing	Capable	Expert
Fluency	Decodes words haltingly	Decodes sentences haltingly	Knows vowel teams (ea, ee, oa, etc.)	Decodes polysyllabic words
	Misses key sounds	Knows conditions for long vowels	Identifies common spelling patterns	Decodes words in context of paragraphs
	Identifies most letter sounds	Identifies blends and consonants	Uses word attack skills to identify new words in the sections	Decodes words accurately and automatically
	Identifies short vowels	Decodes diagraphs and "r" control vowels (or, ar, er, etc.)	Reads sentences in a meaningful sequence	Reads paragraphs in a meaningful sequence
	Says/recognizes individual words	Reads at rate that doesn't interfere with meaning	Reads with expression	Reads with expression, fluency, appropriate tone and pronunciation
Constructive	Predictions are incomplete, partial and unrelated	Predicts what might happen next	Predicts story based upon pictures and other clues	Can predict possible endings to story with some accuracy
	Predictions indicate no or inappropriate prior knowledge	Makes minimal links to personal experience/prior knowledge	Relates story to personal experience/prior knowledge	Can compare/contrast story with personal experience
Motivated	Does not read independently	Reads when parent or teacher requests	Will read for a specific purpose	Initiates reading on own
	Concentrates on decoding	Eager to use the acquired skills (words and phrases)	Uses new skills frequently in self-selected reading	Reads for pleasure
Strategic	Does not self-correct	Recognizes mistakes but has difficulty in self-correcting	Has strategies for self-correction (reread, read ahead, ask a question, etc.)	Analyzes self-correction strategies for the best strategy
	Uncertain as to how parts of a story fit together	Can identify characters and setting in a story	Can identify characters, setting and events of a story	Can talk about story in terms of problem and/or goal
Process	Cannot tell what has been read	Does not sort important from unimportant	What is important and unimportant can be determined with assistance	Organizes reading by sorting important from unimportant

ample, benchmarks are very simple. They identify the critical attributes that students must acquire each six weeks if they are to progress. If the student has not demonstrated these benchmarks, then immediate additional interventions must begin.

How does one get benchmarks? Once again, identify the experienced educators who always have high student achievement. Ask them how they know a student will have trouble. They already know the criteria. And by putting it in writing and having a common understanding, teachers, particularly those who are new to teaching or who are not as experienced, can more readily make interventions and address student progress. It then needs to go back to the grade level for their feedback and changes.

Interventions for Students

The issue here is that the intervention be timely and occur at a classroom and a campus level (see Figure G). One other point is simply that for optimal learning, the student needs to stay with the regular instruction, in as much as possible, to have the opportunity to learn what the other students are learning. Additional time for learning must be found (for example, using social studies time to teach nonfiction reading).

Conclusion

What these systemic interventions allow a campus to do is to address the four variables in learning: 1) the amount of time to learn; 2) the intervention(s) of the teacher; 3) how clear the focus of the instruction is; and 4) what the student came in knowing.

It allows the faculty to address the amount of time, the interventions, the clarity of the instructional focus, and what the student had the opportunity to come in knowing. Right now, because of the depth and breadth of most curriculum guides, it is difficult to

> **"Systemic interventions can identify areas where more time needs to be devoted and can address the effectiveness of both the whole and the component parts of the curriculum."**

Figure F

Benchmarks for fourth-grade language arts
If a student cannot do the following, then immediate interventions need to be used.

First six weeks
• Edit fragments and run-ons in own writing
• Identify and define figurative and literal meaning
• Write an elaborated, organized descriptive paper
• Be able to choose just right books

Second six weeks
• Identify story structure orally and in written form
• Write an organized, elaborated expressive narrative
• Identify correct subject/verb agreement and use in everyday writing
• Use correct pronoun forms in everyday writing

Third six weeks
• Read a passage and use context clues to decode unknown words
• Read a passage and recall facts and details orally and in writing
• Read a story or paragraph and sequence major events
• Write an organized, elaborated how-to

Fourth six weeks
• Read a passage and identify main idea, orally and in written summary
• Read a passage and paraphrase orally and in writing
• Write an organized, elaborated classificatory paper
• Read a passage and identify the best summary
• Write a three to four sentence paragraph

Fifth six weeks
• Use graphic sources to answer questions
• Read passage and predict outcomes and draw conclusions
• Distinguish between fact and nonfact; between stated and nonstated opinion
• After reading a passage, be able to tell cause of an event or effect of an action
• Write an organized, elaborative persuasive paper

Sixth six weeks
• Write an assessment of chosen portfolio pieces
• Assemble/share a reading and writing portfolio

INSTRUCTIONAL
LEADER

Publisher & Education Editor
Sandi Borden

Communications Director
Dorian Martin

Publications Assistant
Cade White

The *Instructional Leader* is published every other month by the Texas Elementary Principals and Supervisors Association, 501 East 10th Street, Austin, Texas 78701. Telephone: (512) 478-5268.

Call for Articles
The *Instructional Leader* welcomes unsolicited submissions; however, it is best to contact Sandi Borden about a topic in advance. For a copy of the writer's guidelines, please contact TEPSA at (512) 478-5268.

printed on recycled paper

Figure G

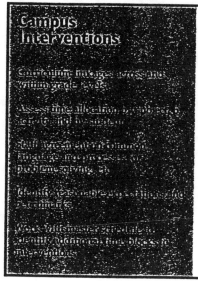

Classroom Interventions
(just a few of many possible)

Goal setting/controlling impulsivity activities

Teaching procedures

Having students write multiple choice questions

Using music to put learning into long-term memory

Increasing the amount of time the student actually reads and writes

Activities that use figural, kinesthetic and symbolic approaches to learning

know what the students actually had the opportunity to learn. By having these systemic items in place, the faculty discussion can truly be data driven; it allows the faculty to talk about student achievement in relationship to the total curriculum.

The discussion can focus on program strengths and weaknesses. It can identify areas where more time needs to be devoted and can address the effectiveness of both the whole and the component parts of the curriculum. It allows a faculty to determine staff development that will address student needs, and it provides one more tool for analyzing TAAS data. Currently, many campuses address the test objective they were low in the year before, only to fall in other objectives the next year. It allows a new teacher to have a much better sense of expectations. Parents have a much better sense of the learning opportunities students will have.

It provides a tool for principals to dialogue with teachers about learning. But more importantly, it allows the campus to identify before the damage is great the students who are not making sufficient progress and to make that intervention immediately, as opposed to one or two years down

the road.

This is the process I used as a principal. Our math scores made significant improvement within two years. I have used it at the secondary level in language arts with excellent results as well.

These simple models and processes give us the tools to talk about what we are doing and to minimize the roller coaster ride for students.

References

Becoming a Nation of Readers. 1984. Center for the Study of Reading. University of Illinois. Champagne, Illinois.

Bloom, Benjamin. 1976. *Human Characteristics and School Learning.* McGraw-Hill. New York, New York.

Fullan, Michael G. 1996. Turning Systemic Thinking on Its Head. *Phi Delta Kappan.* February, 1996, pp. 420-423.

Fullan, Michael G. 1996. *The New Meaning of Educational Change.* Teachers College Press. Columbia University. New York, New York. ❧

Bibliography

Bloom, Benjamin. (1976). *Human Characteristics and School Learning*. New York, NY: McGraw-Hill Book Company.

Caine, Renate Nummela, & Caine, Geoffrey. (1991). *Making Connections: Teaching and the Human Brain*. Alexandria, VA: Association of Supervision and Curriculum Development.

Calallen Middle School. Calallen Independent School District. (1998). Corpus Christi, TX.

Eisner, Elliott, & Vallance, Elizabeth. (1974). *Conflicting Conceptions of Curriculum*. Berkeley, CA: McCutchan Publishing.

Feuerstein, Reuven, et al. (1980). *Instrumental Enrichment: An Intervention Program for Cognitive Modifiability*. Glenview, IL: Scott, Foresman & Company.

Gerzon, Mark. (1996). *A House Divided*. New York, NY: Putnam Publishing Company.

Glickman, Carl, Jordan, Stephan P., & Ross-Gordon, Jovita M. (1997). *Supervision of Instruction: A Developmental Approach* (Fourth Edition). New York, NY: Allyn & Bacon.

Goose Creek Consolidated Independent School District. (1990). Baytown, TX (work shared by district math team).

Goose Creek Consolidated Independent School District. (1994). Baytown, TX (work done in collaboration with Ruby Payne).

Idol, Lorna, & Jones, B.F. (Eds.). (1991). *Educational Values and Cognitive Instruction: Implications for Reform*. Hillsdale, NJ: Lawrence Erlbaum Associates.

Joyce, Bruce, Showers, Beverly, & Rolheiser-Bennett, Carol. (1987). Staff development and student learning: a synthesis of research on models of teaching. *Educational Leadership*. October.

Krupp, Judy-Arin. (1983). *Life Developmental Tasks and Related Learning Needs and Outcomes*. Raleigh, NC: National Society for Internships and Experiential Education.

Lezotte, Lawrence W. (1992). *Creating the Total Quality Effective School*. Okemos, MI: Effective Schools Products.

Runyan Elementary School. Conroe Independent School District. (1996). Conroe, TX (work done in collaboration with Ruby Payne).

http://intranet.cps.k12.il.us/Assessments/Ideas_and_Rubrics/Rubric_Bank/MathRubrics.pdf

www.indep.k12.mo.us/pdc/MAPS/Math8/math_rubric.htm%20copy

www.laramie1.k12.wy.us/instruction
www.laramie1.k12.wy.us/instruction/math/benchmarkmath.htm

Notes

Notes

Notes

Notes

Notes

Notes

Notes

Notes